This book is for

- You don't feel l "salesperson".

- You think selling is about techniques and trickery. (It's actually about good communication and understanding how to communicate).

- Selling is something that confuses or intimidates you.

- You want to understand what makes your clients "tick".

- You want to maximise every opportunity, every client, every communication- but don't know how.

- You want some real world actionable things to change how you sell, right now, today.

You will learn:

- How to engage clients with "Information Gaps".

- Why the Curse of Knowledge can cost you the sale.

- The power of The Von Restorff Effect and Propinquity.

- Why a client's name is so important.

- The Three components needed to make the sale.

- How the False Consensus Effect can cost you every sale you make.

- The common techniques that cause you to buy the things you buy.

....and much more.

Praise for Clear Sales Message:

"The **"little black book"** *of sales."*

"A **straight talking and jargon free** *guide which you can put to work immediately."*

"Clear Sales Message has **transformed how we talk about our business***."*

"Clear Sales Message is **written in plain English** *and is designed to be* **used as a practical manual***, not a reference."*

"Easy to read and implement. **A future business classic.***"*

Understand your buyer:

*"If they don't understand it.
They can't buy it.
But if you don't understand
<u>them,</u> you can't sell it."*

UNDERSTAND YOUR BUYER

About the author

James Newell created Clear Sales Message in 2017 as he transitioned from a **successful career in the corporate sales environment** to finding and following his passion running his own sales consultancy.

Having supplied £600M worth of vehicles to his clients over 12 years and having **never missed a sales target** in that time; James sought to distil the "secrets" that contributed to his performance and to use this to train others.

Working with small to medium size businesses in the UK it became apparent very quickly that many businesses required a defined value proposition- or "sales message".

By creating a means for companies and salespeople to communicate more clearly, James was able to **transform their performance** and also understand just how he performed so well.

It turns out that **selling all comes down to the quality of your communication.**

"Sales is about good communication and finding a connection, not techniques and trickery. If you can clearly articulate what you offer and find those that are in need then you make the sale. Too many sales are lost simply because no-one clearly understands the offering."

"If they don't understand it. They can't buy it." Became the Mantra for Clear Sales Message and something that resonated with clients in the UK and across the world.

Having created online courses, written books and helped countless businesses with their sales messaging, James has firmly found his passion and dedicates his time to educating others as to the power of communication in the sales environment.

www.clearsalesmessage.com

Contents

Introduction

This is a book about understanding your buyer.

It's also a book about understanding **you**.

Although you are reading this book as a seller or salesperson, it makes sense that you are also a buyer.

This is a key point to remember as you read through the book and understand more about how people work, how communication works and how selling communication works. You will recognise some of the elements discussed here in the things that you buy and the way that you are "sold" to.

The reason for this is simple.

This book was created from real world experience and example – not perfect world theory. In doing so we ensure that everything is realistic and workable- there is no perfect world theory here.

In much the same way you don't like how it feels to be pushed into buying or chased, the same is true here. What *feels* right as a seller will feel right as a buyer - they are both sides of the same coin.

Collated into sections for maximum effectiveness, Understand Your Buyer is less of a book and more of a reference tool for you to call upon at various stages of the selling process.

I am always keen to hear about how my readers put these effects into practise so please share your first-hand successes and experiences with me via email:

understandyourbuyer@clearsalesmessage.com.

Are you sitting comfortably......?

How People Work

To play the game, you first need to know the rules.

Understanding how people "work" is at the heart of this book.

Much of what follows looks at specific actions you can take and specific situations that may arise, but there are some specific characteristics about how your buyer's mind operates that are universal. You will know this to be true, because you will recognise much of these behaviours in yourself when you are looking to buy something. Many modern-day companies and advertisers are geared towards making the most of how people "tick".

These first few pages are dedicated to human nature, common sense and basic psychology, so that you understand how your buyers' mind "works".

With this knowledge, you can then alter how and when you communicate; mindful of being noticed and understood.

Let's begin by understanding the basics of how your buyer works...

Confirmation Bias

- ## *Finding "yes" from "no".*

What is it?

The Confirmation Bias is our natural tendency to seek information that supports our thinking, rather than to challenge it.

Why does it work?

If you can communicate with the client from their perspective and confirm their thinking and viewpoint in your sales messaging, you are more likely to engage them and assure them that making the purchase is the right choice for them. The opposite is also true; if you oppose a client's viewpoint and actively criticise them then you are likely to damage rapport and the likelihood of the sale.

How can you use it?

Use plain English terminology that reflects the buyer's thoughts such as "how does this work" to present and link to information. If a prospect was thinking you were expensive and you confirm the thinking and then address it, you are more likely to engage them.

An example

When you ask for an opinion on a favourite movie and everyone chooses Shawshank Redemption (see the Bandwagon Effect for why this happens) but one person hates it and thinks it's only a so-so movie.

In your group and in your mind that person's thoughts are somehow less valid as they do not conform to your enjoyment of the film.

Try this:

If you have a favourite sports team, favourite musician or follow a religion, then start looking for 10 reasons why that team, person or religion is completely wrong and perhaps even a waste of your time.

Notice how difficult it feels to even start thinking about this- let alone Googling it. We find it hard to seek out ideas that oppose our own as it's naturally uncomfortable.

See also:

- How People Work > The False Consensus Effect
- How People Work > The Curse of Knowledge
- How People Work > Emotion Trumps Logic
- How to Engage > Common Enemy Effect
- How to Convert > Social Proof

Sell the Destination

- *Sell the destination, not the journey.*

What is it?

Your buyers primary concern is with the end result they seek. Focussing on the "destination" and end result your clients seek will naturally capture their attention and engage them.

Why does it work?

It works because as human beings we are naturally self-focussed. Your buyers are focussed on their needs and you as a seller are focussed on the details of your offering. By switching focus from what you offer to what that means for the buyer you are "speaking their language" and thus more likely to engage with them.

How can you use it?

Putting this into practise is simple to do, but difficult to remember as your natural inclination is to focus on yourself. When communicating with buyers you need to start with talking about what matters to them most- what are they trying to achieve? what would success look like to them? What's the end result they are trying to achieve?

Once that's established then you can relate that to your offering and how you make it happen.

An example

The best example here would be airline adverts. Airlines use cocktails, families on beaches and romantic views in their advertising. It's actually quite rare their adverts even feature a plane of a plane seat. Airlines understand they need to sell the destination, not the journey (although the "journey" is what they *actually* want you to buy - the actual seat on the plane.)

Try this:

Reverse the order of how you present your offering. Talk about the end result, the benefits, the amazing results and end product FIRST. By talking about this first we can seize buyer attention as we demonstrate we understand their needs and interests. With their attention seized we can then talk about "how" we achieve the end result they seek.

See also:

- How People Work > Emotion Trumps Logic
- Communication Basics > The Framing Effect
- Communication Basics > The Inverted Pyramid
- How to Get Attention > The Before /After Effect
- How to Engage > The Anticipation Effect
- How to Convert > The Ready to Use Effect

WYSIWYG

- *What you see is what you get.*

What is it?

WYSIWYG looks at the fact that we can only process the information we are presented with.

Why does it work?

If you fail to educate your clients about products and services you offer or if you fail to provide them with enough information to make a decision, they may find they simply cannot make a decision. If you don't tell them about something, they won't know about it.

How can you use it?

Are you presenting all of the information you need to, to be able to handle your client's questions and enquiries? Could you share more information, FAQ or proof of success stories to allow your clients to make a more informed decision? You may think you are presenting all the information you need to, but could be missing some fundamental basics which can cost you the sale.

An example

I am sitting in a coffee shop as I write this and the person behind me ordered a coffee with Soya Milk. Nowhere on the menu could I see Soya Milk, but as it was not made obvious to me I presumed it was not available. What I saw was what I got – no Soya milk.

Try this

If you use an iPhone, search online for "tips and tricks" that can be done with the phone. For example, if you want to "undo" some text you shake the phone. There is a ton of functionality but as it is "hidden" we aren't aware of it. For your business, make an effort to mention everything about your offering that matters to your client. After all assumption is the mother of all lost sales.

See also:

- Communication Basics > The Burden of Proof
- Communication Basics > The Inverted Pyramid
- How to Get Attention > The Repetition Effect
- How to Get Attention > Cake Mix Selling
- How to Engage > The Repurposing Effect
- How to Engage > The Education Effect
- How to Convert > The Bare Minimum Effect
- How to Convert > The Checklist Effect

Cognitive Load

- *One thing at a time...*

What is it?

Cognitive Load is about recognising the limited number of things we can pay attention to at any one time. Although we are surrounded by stimulating things throughout the day we can only pay attention to a limited few - this is in part thanks to the something in your brain known as the Reticular Activating System which controls what you focus on.

How does it work?

If you present overly complicated or unclear information to your potential clients, thanks to cognitive load it literally may not be "taken in". Your potential clients may simply not have enough "cognitive load" left to really understand what you are saying.
From overly complicated products to "busy" websites or marketing which lacks direction and a call to action, there are a myriad of ways cognitive overload could be costing you the attention of your potential clients - and thus sales.

How can you use it?

Cognitive load is concerned with how much the brain can do at any one time.

It makes sense that by reducing this load you can capture more attention. This means you simply need to present less information at any one time to ensure it's in a small enough "chunk" for it to be understood.

Two simple techniques to reduce the amount of information you present are:

Use steps

A worked example is essentially a step-by-step demonstration where a process is reduced to single actions, reducing the intrinsic cognitive load resulting from a complex task.

Remove distractions

Identify the necessary words, images and "things" that can be eliminated and have no adverse effect on your potential clients.

An example

This book is the example. There are a lot of ideas in the book, but the only way to communicate them effectively is to arrange them into sections and then each section into paragraphs. To deliver the information any other way may cause confusion and prevent you fully reading or understanding the content.

Try this:

To better communicate with your clients, break down your information into steps and segments and "step" them into the information in logical and formulaic way.
Using "step by step" guides and processes to explain how things work is an accepted and universal way to combat Cognitive Load.

See also:

- How People Work > Decision Fatigue
- How People Work > Overchoice

Decision Fatigue

- *More questions drive poorer decision making.*

What is it?

Decision Fatigue looks at how the quality of our decision making deteriorates the more decisions we have to make.

Why does it work?

The human brain can only process so much information. Making numerous decisions can tax the brain and each subsequent decision becomes more difficult as a result.

How can you use it?

Can you eliminate some of the decision-making elements from your sales process? either by providing "popular" and "recommended" options, or presenting clients with decisions in a sparser manner?

An example

When you are in a restaurant and they hand you a menu, there are often so many choices that it can be difficult to decide what to have. (Just ask my wife...) McDonalds succeed as a "restaurant" because they organise their menu and simplify the choices to make it easier to make a choice.

Try this:

In your own business; if you need your clients to make lots of choices before they can use your offering - try eliminating or grouping some of these choices to make each decision simpler and with less alternatives to "step" the buyer into the information.

See also:

- How People Work > Cognitive Load
- How People Work > Overchoice
- How People Work > Path of Least Resistance

Emotion Trumps Logic

- *If you want to sell, be emotional.*

What is it?

Recognising that your clients are buying the end result, the destination (and not the journey) are everything in sales. When you can get your clients to think about the end result and visualise what that may feel like or what that may mean then you are more likely to create a connection.

How does it work?

Delivering facts and figures and "telling" clients is one thing, but if you only communicate in the logical you may be losing sales. Encourage your clients to experience the end result of your product or service before they have even purchased to create the emotional connection and increase your chances of a sale.

How can you use it?

Emotions are tricky things - especially in the business environment, but making an emotional connection with your clients is essential to driving sales, loyalty and satisfaction. A simple way to do this is visualisation.

Ask your client to imagine what it would be like when they have your product or service and contrast that to the current day. How different is the end result from where they are now and what does that feel like?

An example

It's highly likely that you have joined a gym at some point but not stayed the distance. As much as you want to eat healthily and workout you don't. But why? You logically know and want to be fitter, but your emotions are driving you to stay in bed rather than be at the gym or reward your "hard work" with chocolate because you've worked so hard.

Our emotions of needing a treat overrule or logic that we want to pursue a better body.

Try this:

Use the phrase "this means" to turn a feature into a benefit. Business often sell features and clients buy benefits, to turn a feature of a product into a benefit, you simply need to use the phrase "this means". For example, the Clear Sales Message book is full of useful templates and tools (feature) this means you can create a much clearer sales message.

message yourself and be more confident, but without paying for consultancy. (benefit).

See also:

- How People Work > Confirmation Bias
- How People Work > The Abundance Effect
- How People Work > The Treat Effect
- How People Work > Sell the Destination
- How to Get Attention > The SEX Effect
- How to Get Attention > The Respect Effect
- How to Engage > FOMO
- How to Engage > The Empathy Effect
- How to Engage > The Personification Effect
- How to Engage > Trigger Point
- How to Engage > The User Generated Content Effect

Overchoice

- *Too many choices lead to no choice.*

What is it?

Over choice looks at the fact that the human brain can only process so many options at once, too many decisions and no decision is made as there is "over choice".

Why does it work?

It works because it reminds us to simplify our offering and "step" our clients through the products and services we offer rather than presenting them with a plethora of options. If you present less choices, the client is more likely to make a choice.

How can you use it?

Think about your products and services. Think about your website. Think about your emails. Can you strip away some of the choices & information you communicate completely, or at least split it out so clients receive it in a step-by-step fashion?

An example

If you've ever been to Subway for a sandwich it can be overwhelming and off-putting. Which bread? 6" or 12"? Which sandwich? Which salad? Sauce? Drink? Cookie? I personally like a Subway sandwich but avoid buying because there are just so many choices that it becomes a pain. Contrast this with McDonalds - "which of the 5 meals (which are numbered) would you like?" "Want to make it bigger?" That's it.

Try this:

If there are lots of choice in your offering, what can you eliminate or reduce to get a much simpler and clearer offering? Can you group together common options to create a smaller choice, perhaps even adding numbers or codes as per McDonalds?

See also:

- How People Work > Cognitive Load
- How People Work > Decision Fatigue

Shiny Object Syndrome

- *The newest, shiniest things attract the most attention.*

What is it?

Our tendency as buyers is to prefer the newest, the latest and the most cutting edge things available. There is often a tendency to also be the first or the best (a variation on The Exclusive Effect)

Why does it work?

By focussing on the latest and newest aspects of your offering you will appeal to those "early adopters" and potential clients who like to be ahead of their peers.
These people don't mind buying things sometimes even if they are unproven – so long as they are first. Sometimes people buy things to be first, but also just to stop others having them - especially things in limited supply such as domain names.

How can you use it?

Describe your offering using words ending in "est" – newest, fastest, shiniest, bestest etc.
Focus on how your offering will put your potential clients ahead of their peers. Focus on how your

offering is the latest, greatest and most advanced use of science, art, technology, etc.

If your buyers believe they have the opportunity to buy the newest, bestest most shiniest widget, then it can be a closing factor and move them to buy.

An example

Each year Apple launch new versions of the iPhone. Whilst some new technology is introduced, there isn't much difference in an iPhone 6,7 or 8 and yet people camp out overnight to secure the latest handset and to be the first.

Try this:

Think about something you want to treat yourself to that perhaps you can't afford. Go to eBay and find the same item. It will be used but much cheaper than buying new. If you want the item so much, then buying it cheaper on eBay is a no brainer - so, why don't you? Because the item is second hand, isn't shiny, isn't brand new and may have some signs of wear and tear. You are more likely to not buy it cheaper and wait to buy the new version or buy the new version on credit.

The reason? You want the "thing" to be shiny, new and all yours – not something that someone has already used. This is also an example of emotion trumping logic which drives much of your buyer's behaviour.

See also:

- How to Get Attention > The NEW Effect
- How to Get Attention > The New Version Effect
- How to Get Attention > The Award-Winning Effect
- How to Convert > The Early Bird Effect
- How to Convert > The First Purchase Effect
- How to Convert > The Trade in Effect

Path of Least Resistance

- *The easier you are to deal with, the easier it is to buy from you.*

What is it?

The Path of Least Resistance is the natural tendency for people to take the easiest option / most direct route to their destination or to solve their needs.

Why does it work?

If we recognise that our potential clients are seeking the easiest, fastest solution we can tailor what we do accordingly, removing blockers and unnecessary elements. Companies such as McDonalds and Amazon base their entire model on a systemised process focussed on being as easy to deal with as possible.

How can you use it?

Adopting your client's perspective, how would you want your product or service to operate? Ask yourself: What would make you easier to deal with? How could you work faster or more efficiently?

An example

In your neighbourhood, there will almost certainly be pathways next to grass and paths that have been cut through the grass by people walking across it. These are known as "wander lines". Where the pavement contractors think everyone walks in straight lines and right angles, real world people cut across grass and pavement to make the shortest route possible. This is a real-world example of a basic human phenomenon - we always take the easiest, simplest, quickest route to our destination.

Try this:

The next time you need a book, or to buy ANYTHING from Amazon, don't do it and go to a real-world shop to make the purchase. Notice how much more time, energy and money you will spend in doing so - for seemingly no return whatsoever. Amazon in particular have made purchasing from them so easy and favourable that it's a no brainer to purchase anywhere else.
This is happening for your business and with your competitors. Are you easier to buy from than the competition? Could you remove any complication, cost or steps to emulate the Amazon simplicity model? Try buying from yourself- how difficult is it?

See also:

- How People Work > Decision Fatigue
- How People Work > The Local Effect
- How People Work > The Guessing Game
- Communication Basics > Clustering
- How to Get Attention > The Show and Tell Effect
- How to Get Attention > Cake Mix Selling
- How to Engage > The Speed Effect
- How to Convert > The Deal Effect
- How to Convert > The Finance Effect
- How to Convert > The No Brainer Effect
- How to Convert > The Comparison Effect
- How to Convert > The Freedom Effect
- How to Convert > The Kids Go Free Effect
- How to Convert > The With-Purchase Effect
- How to Convert > The Mini Pack Effect
- How to Convert > The Ready to Use Effect

See also: Psychology of Price

The numbers you use in your pricing can have an impact on The Path of Least Resistance and make the buying decision easier or more difficult.

The False Consensus Effect

- *Perception is 9/10s of the law.*

What is it?

The False Consensus Effect is the false belief that
other people see the world in the same way we do.
The reality is that we all have differing viewpoints,
so to engage we need to think about the other
person and seek to understand them.

Why does it work?

The False Consensus Effect can disconnect us
from our clients as it blocks engaged
communication. Addressing the False Consensus
Effect can increase our chances of engaging and
converting clients as we communicate with them in
a manner which recognises and validates their
perspective.

How can you use it?

Adopting your client's point of view and tailoring
your message accordingly increases engagement.
Use real world examples of other clients in similar
positions that you have helped, adopt client
terminology and research their motivations to
demonstrate you understand and you care.

An example

I'm sitting in a café as I write this. The person that served me my coffee has a different viewpoint on the coffee shop than I do. I see this as a calm peaceful place to work - they may see it as an unhappy place they bear to make money. Two people in the same place can have completely different viewpoints.

Try this:

Sit with a friend or partner and pick a shared experience you have had together. Both write down your memory of the experience and the most notable parts. Then share what you have written and notice the differences.

This is happening right now for your business. Read reviews and seek feedback from your clients to get an insight into how your business and offering are **really** perceived and understood – if it doesn't match your own perception then you'll need to bridge the gap to engage with future clients.

See also:

- How People Work > Confirmation Bias
- How People Work > The Curse of Knowledge
- How to Engage > First Person Questions

The Law of Past Experience

- *Preconceptions can help or hinder the sale.*

What is it?

The Law of Past Experience recognises that your potential clients will have preconceived ideas and understanding about your offering - both good and bad.

Why does it work?

Understanding the negative points so you can counter them and understanding the positives so you can harness them will put you ahead in any sales conversation.

How can you use it?

When speaking with your client it's important to ask them questions and seek to understand their opinion and past experience of products and services like yours or in the same arena. Once you understand if there is a past experience and whether its positive or negative, you can then use this in your ongoing sales interaction.

An example

How do you feel about car salespeople? Or estate agents? You will have ingrained feelings about these people in your mind based on past experience and/or the opinions of others. The same may be true of your business or profession.

Try this:

Revisit a restaurant where you've had a bad experience or try listening again to that album you just didn't like. Through more "exposure" can you overcome your natural aversion and actually enjoy the experience?
This will be the same for your clients, so it's vital you understand if they have any dealings with your type of business/offering before and if it was positive or negative. That past experience will help or hinder your relationship with the client.

See also:

- How People Work > The Curse of Knowledge
- How People Work > Emotion Trumps Logic
- How to Engage > Common Enemy Effect
- How to Engage > The Premium Effect
- How to Engage > The Education Effect
- How to Engage > The Nostalgia Effect

The Curse of Knowledge

- *It's difficult to "unlearn" things.*

What is it?

The Curse of Knowledge is our inability to "un-know" things once we know them. Once we have a fixed understanding or viewpoint on something, it can be very difficult to change it.

Why does it work?

Once we know and understand something we often stay stuck to that perspective. This works for you if you can educate your clients about your products and services to set their knowledge point, but can work against you if your clients have a negative view towards your offering.

How can you use it?

If you want to engage with your clients, sometimes you need to challenge their thinking. Is there a particular stigma, opinion or thought about your product or service? If so, can you confront this "Curse of Knowledge" head on to engage your buyer and to change their perception?

Our work at Clear Sales Message can sometimes be considered to be "The Emperor's New Clothes" as there is a level of intangibility to the services we provide. As such, there is a page in our book entitled "Isn't this all the Emperor's New Clothes?". By tackling this potential issue head on, we seize attention, deal with the issue and exude confidence as it's a bold move.

An example

What if I told you that your car keys have travelled further than your car ever has? Seems odd, doesn't it? but as you walk around with your car keys in your bag or pocket you rack up mileage without your car being there.
This simple and obvious statement is unexpected and more likely to stay in your mind. It's hard to "un-know" that your keys have travelled more than your car ever will once you know.

Try this:

Go to YouTube and look at a "behind the scenes" video for your favourite magic trick. You know, the one that's always baffled you...
Watch the video to see how it's done and then watch the trick being performed properly. Never again will you be able to watch the trick and enjoy the "magic"- you will be thinking about how the trick is "really" done.

See also:

- How People Work > Confirmation Bias
- How People Work > The False Consensus Effect
- How People Work > The Law of Past Experience
- How People Work > Emotion Trumps Logic

The Local Effect

- ***Supporting the local community is always attractive.***

What is it?

We are more likely to engage with and buy from businesses that are nearer to us than farther away. Focussing on the location of your business in your messaging can be a deciding factor for potential buyers

Why does it work?

It works because we value speed and convenience when looking to purchase something (Path of Least Resistance). A more local supplier means a quicker delivery or less travel time which are more appealing. Local businesses can also imply a local expertise, knowledge and trust over a more "faceless" corporate alternative.

How can you use it?

Depending on the nature of your business, referencing the geographical location you serve will help to engage and convert more clients. Include your location and focus area in your marketing and on your website to reassure those in the locality that you are the preferred choice for "locals".

An example

You need to purchase something that you forgot in the "big shop". Rather than travel all the way to the main supermarket you use, you will have to buy that item (at a likely higher price) from the local shop. Your need for speed and convenience - dictated by location – have sealed the deal.

Try this:

The next time you need to buy something, visit your local shops instead of the supermarket and notice the difference in terms of the relationships you can form with your local community. Saving money and convenience are one thing, but supporting small business is something we all need to consider.

See also:

- How People Work > The Path of Least Resistance
- How to Engage > The Patriotic Effect

The Established Effect

- *The longer you've been doing it, the better.*

What is it?

The amount of time you have been in business can be a deciding factor for your potential buyers.

Why does it work?

It works because it implies success, stability and reliability. There is a reason you have been in business for 2,322 years....
As buyers, we want to make a safe and secure choice and if you have been in business for a long time then you must be doing something right.

How can you use it?

If your business has been around for 5/10/20/30 or more years, then using this in your messaging encourages trust and implies stability.

An example

At your local dentist, you know Bob and have been going there for years, Bob takes good care of you and your teeth. Today Bob's apprentice Steve is going to be working on your teeth; under Bob's supervision.

You know Steve has only just qualified and this is his second full time day – do you feel comfortable with him working on you? Of course not. His lack of experience will worry you in the same way a lack of experience can affect your potential buyers.

Try this:

If your business was established a while ago, start to incorporate this into your marketing and website. Publicise anniversaries such as 10/15/20 years since you were established. You will attract more clients who weren't aware what a safe bet you are.

See also:

- How to Engage > The Heritage Effect
- How to Engage > The Nostalgia Effect
- Communication Basics > Confidence. Certainty. Expertise.

The Abundance Effect

- *We like to buy more than we need.*

What is it?

We are more likely to buy things that include lots of items because it feels like better value for money because we are getting "more".

Why does it work?

It works because as buyers we are always looking for the best deals and the best value. An offer which has 25/50/100pcs or a service with a long bullet point list or lots of sections is more appealing as we are getting more and thus it must be better value.
Often we don't need or use these extra items, but are happy to have them anyway and don't feel like we've wasted our money because you never know when you might need them...

What can you do about it?

Whether you have a product or service, consider itemising every single part of your offering and go into as much detail as possible. This extra detail will encourage buyers that they are getting "a lot" for their money and will increase the chances they will buy.

An example

If you have a Sky TV subscription at home, you get access to hundreds of channels, or if you have Netflix / Spotify, you have access to millions of films and songs. How many films, channels or songs do you watch in a week? Or a month? Chances are the thought of having access to all that entertainment sold you on the subscription, but some days may pass where you don't watch a single film, TV program or listen to a song. Despite that, you feel justified in buying as you have access to all that entertainment.... if and when you need it.

Try this:

The next time you find a "buy one get one free" deal in a shop, buy one but decline the free one. The person serving you at the till will almost certainly bring this to your attention and think you're crazy to forego something for free. Even if you don't need the extra free item, not accepting something for "free" seems illogical to most.

See also:

- How People Work > Emotion Trumps Logic
- How People Work > The Unlimited Effect
- How People Work > The ""In for a Penny"" Effect
- How to Convert > The Mega Pack Effect
- How to Convert > The No Brainer Effect
- How to Convert > The Checklist Effect

The Unlimited Effect

- *We are attracted to no restrictions and no limits- even if we don't use them.*

What is it?

We are more likely to buy things that are "unlimited" rather than those which have a fixed amount of supply - even if we have no need and will not utilise more than the "limited" offering.

Why does it work?

It works because as buyers we are seeking not only the best value which is often identified by sheer quantity of the offering, but we are also looking to minimise our risk. An offering which is unlimited can seemingly have no downside as we can use as much as we need.
The reality is that "unlimited" offers seldom get a lot of usage, but it's the peace of mind that "unlimited" provides that can help to convert the sale.

What can you do about it?

If part of your offering can be made "unlimited"

and it has no real affect to your bottom line, then this can be a powerful addition to your sales pitch. Digital products and intangible items can be made unlimited quite easily and for no cost, with a potentially *unlimited* upside.

An example

Do you have unlimited calls and texts on your mobile phone plan? Most phone companies offer this now which seems incredibly generous and helps justify the monthly cost. But check your *actual* usage each month- I send less that 50 text messages in a month, but the lure of "unlimited" feels great for that one month I might just need to send 1,000 text messages....

Try this:

In terms of consumption, there is always a limit. Selling "unlimited" anything is misleading as you will never truly use everything on offer. Visit a Chinese all you can eat buffet and rather than piling your plate high and making multiple trips - fill one plate, eat it and leave. Feel how strange it is to leave all of that "free" food there and not take advantage of unlimited supply.

See also:

- How People Work > The Abundance Effect
- How to Convert > The Buy More Effect

The "In for a Penny" Effect

- *If you're doing it, you might as well do it properly.*

What is it?

The "In for a Penny" Effect describes the process of rationalising a larger purchase once you have already decided to buy. It comes from the phrase "In for a Penny. In for a pound."

Why does it work?

It works because once we have decided to buy, we are desensitised to the money we are spending and now "invested" in the purchase. If we've already rationalised spending £x, then the leap from £x to £xx is now a smaller and easier jump to make. Motivated by FOMO (Fear of Missing Out) and loss aversion we increase what we're spending, hoping to achieve the best outcome possible. After all, if we're spending a penny, we may as well spend a pound and do it right.

How can you use it?

How can you get your clients to engage in a purchase and then offer them a superior alternative or upgrade once they have already decided to buy?
This is where having a "deal" approach with options can work well indeed as you are simply moving the buyer from one package to the next.

An example

Many Fast Food chains price their burgers high and their meals low which makes the jump from burger to meal seem a no brainer. If you are spending £3 on a burger, then you may as well spend £4.30 and get fries and a drink as well. After all, the drink alone is £2 so spending more here is a bargain.... Isn't it?

Try this:

The next time you offer something for sale, make the "upsell" of that offering only marginally more expensive if possible. By creating a smaller gap, you will encourage buyers to choose a more expensive option than stick with the cheapest possible option.

See also:

- How People Work > The Abundance Effect
- How to Convert > The Buy More Effect

The Treat Effect

- *We all deserve a little treat now and again.*

What is it?

The Treat Effect recognises that as human beings we often feel entitled to and deserving of many things which we don't have. By appealing to this desire to "spoil" or "indulge" we can display empathy and increase our chances of making the sale.

Why does it work?

Life is tough. We work long hours, get up early, go to bed late, try to eat well, exercise, save money, spend time with loved ones, have time alone, decorate, exercise, learn, grow, travel....
You get the picture.
In our world of excess and overwhelm we can lose ourselves as people and feel like we are doing everything for everyone else and nothing for ourselves.
The Treat Effect recognises this imbalance and encourages our potential clients to act on their urge to put themselves first "for a change".

How can you use it?

By recognising the pressures of your potential client and the fact that they often don't come first, you can make it clear that you understand. Painting a picture of their stressful life where everyone else seems to come first and contrasting that with indulging in your product or service because they "deserve it" confirms that perhaps it is time to spend some time and attention closer to home.

An example

Think about the last time you ordered a takeaway or had a few drinks at home. Was it because you had a busy and stressful week and you're trying to "unwind". Think about how you justify the unnecessary purchases you make in terms of how much you need a treat or how hard you have worked. This is the Treat Effect in action.

Try this:

The next time you want to treat yourself to something as you have been working hard, tired or feel you deserve it. Stop. Experiment with what happens if you fight the urge to treat yourself and how it makes you feel.

See also:

- How People Work > Emotion Trumps Logic
- How to Engage > The Empathy Effect
- How to Convert > The Gift Effect

The Authority Effect

- *Monkey see. Monkey do.*

What is it?

The Authority Effect occurs when we are compelled to do something because we have been told to by a person of authority, or have simply witnessed that person doing the same.
A person of authority can be a celebrity, a peer or someone successful in your space that you look up to and aspire to be like.

Why does it work?

It's a form of social proof. We want to do things that are tried, test, approved and we want to identify with people who are like us. The effect is so powerful that by a celebrity simply wearing a certain type of watch can mean we are compelled to want it - they don't even need to explicitly endorse it.

How can you use it?

The Authority Effect can apply to every business, but isn't feasible for every business. You need to have access to well known or successful people who have some form of influence over them followers and audience. If you do have access to someone of influence, then you can ask them to directly recommend your offering, or simply be seen to be using it.

An example

When someone famous such as The Duchess of Cambridge wears a particular dress, it's sold out online in minutes. Without an explicit endorsement, simply wearing something can cause others to want to buy it as they want to "be like" the Duchess.

Try this:

Think about the watch you own, the car you drive, the products you buy. It's almost guaranteed that you will have made at least one of those purchases as the result of seeing a celebrity endorsement and identifying with that person's image. Be mindful of the things you want and the things you buy – often your desire is heightened by The Authority Effect.

See also:

- How to Engage > The Should Effect
- How to Engage > The Because Effect
- How to Engage > The "I have a Dream" Effect
- How to Convert > The Refer a Friend Effect
- How to Convert > Social Proof

See also: Psychology of Colour

The colours you use to evoke trust can have an impact on your buyer and drive their engagement and decision making. Blue is often recommended as a "trustworthy" colour.

The Guessing Game

- *Help your clients connect the dots.*

What is it?

The Guessing Game reminds us that most potential clients are trying to connect the dots from their limited understanding of your offering. As such they will guess where appropriate and seek to make their own conclusions.

Why does it work?

It works because this is at the very heart of sales messaging. In as few words as possible you need to convey your offering, intrigue and engage. In much the same way a dot to dot creates a picture, you need to consider how the information you communicate about your business builds up to make the overall picture.

How can you use it?

The acid test is can you stop someone in the street and try to explain to them what you do in as few words as possible? How would you do it? What would you say? What information could you provide that when connected together will create the picture of your actual offering? Saying your offering is like something else (Equivalence) and being clear to cover the obvious details (WYSIWYG) are a great starting point.

An example

The title of this book is an example of the Guessing Game in action. In 3 words "Understand Your Buyer" we can allude to what the book is about, what you can expect and if you'd like to buy it. How could you reduce the complexity of your messaging to the point where if you stopped someone in the street they could guess what you did or what you offered from just a couple of words or a sentence?

Try this:

The next time you get a promotional email from a company - see if you can guess what you think they are offering by skimming the email as quickly as possible. Go back and read the email to see what the real message is and notice the difference in the two. Our perception on "filling in the gaps" can cause us to reach false conclusions very quickly but as buyers this is often how we think.

See also:

- How People Work > The Path of Least Resistance
- How People Work > WYSIWYG
- Communication Basics > The Burden of Proof
- Communication Basics > Clustering

- How to Get Attention > The Ambiguity Effect
- How to Engage > Information Gaps

Communication Basics

The building blocks of all communication.

With an understanding of the basics of how your buyer's mind (and your mind) works, we can then move on to some of the basics of how to actually communicate with clients at all stages of the buying process.

Selling is about good communication and finding a connection point - not techniques and trickery. When we increase the quality of our communication we increase the quality of our selling conversations and the likelihood of sale.

These basics are concerned with when and how to present information to a potential client. They can seize attention, engage and convert, but they are predominantly how we as humans communicate in a sales conversation.

These are the building blocks of all successful selling conversations...

Burden of Proof

- ***It's up to you to "sell" what you offer.***

What is it?

The Burden of Proof reminds us that for us to get clients to buy, we need to do everything possible to give them the information and opportunity to do so. The burden is on us as to whether they buy or not.

Why does it work?

Remembering that we need to provide all of the information, opportunity and ease of interaction required to secure a sale drives our behaviour in the right direction.

How can you use it?

If you were the buyer of your product or service, what questions, fears and uncertainties would you face? Can you find all of the information you need on the product, packaging or website? or is it a couple of clicks deep?
Remembering that The Burden of Proof, the burden of presenting the case to buy what you sell

falls to you, you will avoid falling into the trap of being a "victim" and blaming your clients' lack of understanding or action.

It's all on you to make the sale.

An example

If you've ever been in a conversation where your friend or partner is trying to convince you to do something or go somewhere you will have almost certainly put the focus on them to prove why what they are saying is true. It's the "go-on then... convince me" attitude that your buyers will have and it's up to you to answer all of their questions and allay their fears.

Try this:

The next time you are in a selling conversation or creating sales content; consider that you are putting forward a legal case as to why that person should buy your offering. What is your argument? Your angle? What evidence can you utilise? Do you have any witnesses who can write statements as to how good your offering is?

See also:

- How People Work > The Guessing Game
- How People Work > WYSIWYG
- Communication Basics > The Inverted Pyramid
- Communication Basics > The Facts and Figures Effect

Clustering

- ***Grouping things together aides understanding.***

What is it?

Clustering is the act of collating together similar things- such as information – so that they can be better understood.

Why does it work?

It works because it makes your information easier to digest and understand. By ensuring related items are kept together, you are more likely to keep the reader's attention as the topics are variations on a theme.

How can you use it?

Whenever you present information to a potential client- especially a list – collate the similar information together to allow your recipient a greater chance of understanding. After all, The Burden of Proof is on you.

An example

This book is the example here. Each page is split into sections to allow you to navigate simply and find the information you need. If this book was page after page of long form unbroken text it would be less engaging and worse than that it would fail you, as the reader, as you can't easily find what you need.

Try this:

Next time you email a client or present a lot of information, group it into sections and curate the information to allow your reader to access what they need in a simple and logical fashion.

See also:

- How People Work > The Path of Least Resistance
- How People Work > The Guessing Game
- How to Get Attention > The Hashtag Effect

Positive Feedback Loop

- *Reward behaviour and it is likely to be repeated.*

What is it?

A Positive Feedback Loop is about conditioning behaviour which means rewarding someone to encourage that behaviour. It's like dog training - the more treats they get, the more they take the action that leads to the treat.

Why does it work?

It works because we believe that the past influences the future. If I took action X and got outcome Y before, then why would that not be the same every time?
We carry out reinforced and rewarded behaviour in the hopes of the same reward. Ironically even if the reward is lacking we will still try believing we will be rewarded.

How can you use it?

Supermarkets use this in their loyalty schemes - the more you shop with us, the more you will be rewarded...

Using positive feedback loops in your business means creating a way to positively reward your clients - perhaps with free gifts, loyalty schemes, money off vouchers or other special and unexpected touches.

Once these people come to expect the reward, they have been conditioned to act and are more likely to repeat their behaviour.

An example

The most obvious example here is gambling. When we gamble and win, our behaviour is reinforced and thus we continue to gamble. Even though the reward might be 1 in 100 coins of the roulette wheel, the fact that we have been rewarded drives our behaviour.

Try this

The next time you want someone to do something at work, establish clearly to them what the reward is. It could be something as simple as a chocolate bar or the fact that you will make them their next tea. It doesn't matter. When you reward behaviour, and are clear on the reward offered, people are more likely to act.

See also:

- How to Convert > The Points Effect
- How to Convert > The Loyalty Effect
- How to Convert > The Buy More Effect
- How to Engage > Lagniappe

Schemas

- *How to describe something.*

What is it?

Schemas are the fancy way of saying that we associate characteristics or thoughts with certain things. Using descriptive words and characteristics can help to better explain your offering.

Why does it work?

It works because it provides some context and some familiar terms to help clients to better understand your offering. If your clients understand the characteristics of your offering on their own terms, they can create their own image and understanding in their mind.

How can you use it?

How can you describe your offering in a more contextual way using the power of Schemas using imagery and characteristics? Could you draw comparisons with other things and use equivalence to help explain your offering?

An example

If I say Red, fast, sporty – you think of a car almost certainly, and a sports car at that. What words and characteristics associate with your offering that you can put together in the same way?

Try this:

Pick the most important and obvious physical and experiential characteristics of your offering to explain it.

See also:

- Communication Basics > The Chinese Whisper Effect
- How to Get Attention > The Show and Tell Effect
- How to Get Attention > The Hashtag Effect

Confidence. Certainty. Expertise.

- ***What your clients are <u>really</u> buying.***

What is it?

As buyers, we are looking for three things from the person selling to us. We need to see that they are confident in the delivery of their offering and that they are certain they can solve our problem or meet our need. Finally, we need to be reassured that they are the expert - they have the knowledge, contacts and experience to make it all happen - it's not their first time.

Why does it work?

It works because as buyers we are "in need". Whether it's solving a problem, meeting a need or changing something in our world- we are reaching out for "help" and as such we want the person helping us to be capable of doing so.

How can you use it?

When in conversation with a potential client, or in ANY form of communication with them you need to remember the 3 principles of Confidence, Certainty and Expertise – these are the "hidden" elements that are implied in your communications and not explicitly communicated.

Ask yourself if you are confident, certain and displaying expertise when you communicate - if you are missing even one element it could drastically change the direction of the conversation.

An example

Think of a time when you just haven't felt right about something. The product or service works well and is in your price range, but there is something about the company or salesperson that doesn't add up. It just doesn't feel right...It doesn't matter how great your offering is, you must deliver it in a confident way to assure the buyer that you can take care of their needs and that you are a "safe bet" Any hesitation, any hint of lack of confidence and it can cost you the sale.

Try this:

In any sales conversation, remember that you have to be in the lead. This doesn't mean you talk the most, but it does mean that you shape the conversation and are in control.

See also:

- How People Work > The Established Effect
- How to Get Attention > The Named Process Effect
- How to Get Attention > The Before / After Effect
- How to Engage > First Person Questions
- How to Engage > The Scoring Effect
- How to Convert > The Also Bought Effect
- How to Convert > Social Proof
- How to Convert > The Ready to Use Effect

The Framing Effect

- *Change the context of what you are talking about.*

What is it?

The Framing Effect states that we perceive things differently when they are in a different context.

Why does it work?

When you take something out of context you can see it differently. A Ferrari on the motorway is a special thing, but a Ferrari at a Ferrari Owners Club meeting in a field of hundreds of them, is perceived differently. The car itself is the same, but when the surroundings change it can affect how we perceive it.

How can you use it?

Take your offering and reframe it into a new context. This could be presenting new ways to use your product or service, new benefits it provides or problems it solves. Anything that will change the natural perception of your offering will work.

An example

When you are speaking with a client about your
offering, reframe it's benefits and effects over the
longer term if applicable. 1 month, 1 year, 10 years
from now what will the benefit be from using your
offering? As buyers and sellers, we focus on the
here and now and forget the much longer term
which is where the magic of compounding occurs
to amplify our results.

Try this:

The next time you speak with a client, try
reframing your offering to a new context to change
their perception. The most effective way to do this
is with price. This book costs £15. Compare that to
other books which are £4.99 and it may seem
expensive, but compare it to the results you will
get from implementing the ideas and your £15
investment suddenly feels like a bargain.
Comparing this book to paying £300 for an online
course with the same content has the same effect.
Reframe your offering and you change perception.

See also:

- How People Work > Sell the Destination
- How to Get Attention > The Before /After Effect
- How to Get Attention > The Price Per Use Effect
- How to Engage > The Story Effect
- How to Engage > Equivalence
- How to Convert > The Gift Effect
- How to Convert > The Comparison Effect
- How to Convert > The Mini Pack Effect

The Honesty Effect

- *Honesty is the best policy.*

What is it?

The Honesty Effect involves being up front, open and honest with clients at all times – especially surrounding your flaws and shortcomings.

Why does it work?

If someone is honest with us and shares their imperfections, we are more likely to be endeared to them and to trust them. If you have obvious faults and flaws that will be discovered anyway its best to get them into the open and out of the way rather than hoping they might go un-noticed.

How can you use it?

In your sales pitches and sales copy you can mention minor flaws and imperfections and then counter them with the positive. So, for example your delivery times might be slightly higher than average but every parcel is delivered when it's stated to be there and everything is insured and tracked. By being honest up front you have the opportunity to diffuse any potential negative situations than if (in this instance) the parcel was unexpectedly late the client complains and you are on the back foot.

An example

As a consultant, I am an expert on sales messaging and communication, but not sales strategy. When clients ask me to create a strategy for them I politely decline. It's not my area of expertise. I could take the work and "try" to do it, but risking a poor result and my reputation for any amount of money isn't something I am willing to do. My clients respect my honesty and don't think any less of me. We all know where we stand.

Try this:

Identify the weak points in your offering - the things you get asked to do and don't feel 100% about delivering on. Try refusing that work and explaining its outside your area of expertise or your offering. Not only will your client appreciate your honesty, you will feel better and you won't be risking your reputation delivering sub-standard results you know you shouldn't be delivering in the first place.

See also:

- Communication Basics > Confidence. Certainty. Expertise.
- How to Get Attention > The Respect Effect
- How to Get Attention > Propinquity
- How to Engage > The Empathy Effect

The Inverted Pyramid

- *Start with the most important information when you communicate.*

What is it?

The Inverted Pyramid describes the need to present the most important information first to seize attention.

Why does it work?

It works because human beings have an 8 second attention span. "Cutting to the chase" as quickly as possible is your best chance of seizing this attention and engaging with your potential client.

How can you use it?

If you want to drive engagement with readers of your content or potential clients, find the most important information (important to your client) and present that first. At Clear Sales Message, we describe this as "selling the destination, not the journey". This describes the fact that airlines often don't advertise seats on their airplanes, they advertise the destination. As holiday makers, we care first about where we are going and then about how we will get there.

An example

Amazon is the example here. Amongst the myriad of benefits they offer - fast and free delivery is one of the most important to us as buyers. As such, every listing and every page of their website talks about free delivery over £20 (in the UK). They ensure that the factor most important to us - speed and convenience - is always in the forefront of our minds as they know this is a powerful lever to help us buy.

Try this:

What is the most important part of your offering? Is it the result you deliver? The fact you are award winning, accredited or can deliver in 24hrs? Whatever the most important part of your offering is (most important to your buyer and their needs that is) make sure that is one of the first things on your website, sales literature and in your conversations.

See also:

- How People Work > WYSIWYG
- How People Work > Sell the Destination
- Communication Basics > The Burden of Proof
- How to Get Attention > The Show and Tell Effect
- How to Engage > The Anticipation Effect
- How to Engage > The Scoring Effect

The Facts and Figures Effect

- ***Facts, figures and proof help to convert.***

What is it?

People use facts and figures to influence their buying behaviour – even if the facts and figures are from a dubious source or not even verified. The mere existence of a fact can encourage a client to purchase.

Why does it work?

It works because we believe that facts and figures are generally trustworthy and come from a genuine source. We can abdicate the need to think or justify our actions if we know that xx% of people found a product to be useful or that xx% of situations call for XX product.

How can you use it?

Which genuine - and they must be genuine - facts and figures can you use to help promote your products and services? Could you find some existing research or conduct your own to create

facts and figures that will help you to promote your offering?
For example, 54% of businesses do not have a refined value proposition.

https://blog.hubspot.com/marketing/write-value-proposition

An example

The human attention span is just 8 seconds. This fact helps greatly when communicating the importance of developing a Clear Sales Message and communicating clearly about your offering. Every 8 seconds you are looking for something more interesting to focus on - so it's important to fight for that attention when you are trying to sell.

Try this:

Do your research and see what relevant facts and figures you can find that pertain to your clients and your offering. Credible facts and figures from credible sources about matters that are important to your client can help drive them to buy.

See also:

- How People Work > WYSIWYG
- Communication Basics > The Burden of Proof
- How to Get Attention > The Ambiguity Effect
- How to Get Attention > The Award-Winning Effect
- How to Engage > The Scoring Effect

The Chinese Whisper Effect

- *Your sales message will change as it is transferred.*

What is it?

The quality and content of your sales message will change as it's relayed from person to person. However strong or clear your messaging is, you can't help the fact that people will forget and edit parts of your messaging as it travels.

Why does it work?

Chinese Whispers are human nature; you can't stop it happening. It works because we are only paying so much attention to the things we come across and view the world from our own unique perspective. As such, our recollection of sales messaging reflects this diversity.

What can you do about it?

Using taglines, acrostics and other techniques you can ensure that your sales messaging is not only C.L.E.A.R and more memorable, but that it's the same every time which is the real "secret" to having a Clear Sales Message.

An example

You were told last week about Barry who works in I.T, he focusses on producing strategies to help businesses to become profitable overtime and harness the power of technology. He's had some amazing success and his company is about to be bought by Microsoft.

How do you relay this to your friends? "I met a guy called Barry - works in I.T, Microsoft are about to buy his company." Very little about what he does will shine through, you naturally focus on the most "newsworthy" elements which sadly won't help Barry sell anymore as no-one knows what he offers...

Try this:

When communicating about your offering, you can "seed" words into your buyer's minds for them to repeat to ensure the message isn't lost. If you don't have one, consider creating a catchy tagline - they are one of the most effective methods to get remembered and to combat against The Chinese Whisper Effect.

See also:

- Communication Basics > Schemas
- How to Get Attention > The Named Process Effect
- How to Get Attention > The Jingle Effect
- How to Engage > First Person Questions

- How to Convert > The Refer a Friend Effect

Taglines are a powerful way to help retain your client's engagement and understanding as your message moves from person to person:

www.howtowriteatagline.com

The Timely Effect

- *Timely things are more engaging and front of mind.*

What is it?

Capitalising on a timely event or good news story by changing your messaging can help bring attention to your offering.

Why does it work?

It works because when something captures the public's imagination (such as the wedding of Prince Harry to Meghan Markle) then anything related to that will stand out and be more relatable as it's familiar and timely. This is also taking advantage of Propinquity - people are familiar with the news story or event and you are capitalising on that familiarity.

What can you do about it?

To make this work requires speed and agility. It's about relating your offering to a good news story or timely event. This is only truly successful when the event is on a much larger scale such as the Olympics or a Royal wedding. Keep your eyes peeled for a good news story that captures the public's imagination and then consider how you can relate your offering to that story. But beware the Spam Effect which is about connecting completely unrelated stories to your offering.

An example

Marks and Spencer's or "Marks and Sparks" in the UK changed the signage on their Windsor shop to "Markle and Sparkle" for the Royal wedding and it made the international news: https://metro.co.uk/2018/05/18/ms-change-name-markle-sparkle-royal-wedding-weekend-7556062/

Try this:

What good news or timely event is happening or will happen that you can use to bring attention to your offering. Pancake day? Mother's Day? Christmas? Summer? Winter? Moon landings? Think about how largescale news events (that are 100% positive) can be relayed to your offering. It might just help you get on the international news...

See also:

- Communication Basics > The Themed Sale Effect
- How to Get Attention > Propinquity
- How to Get Attention > The Christmas Effect
- How to Get Attention > The Events Effect
- How to Convert > The Happy Hour Effect

The I/We Effect

- *It's not all about you.*

What is it?

The I/We Effect looks at the difference in connection and engagement between using the word "I" and the word "we" in a sales conversation. Using "we" in early sales conversations has been proven to perform better.

Why does it work?

It works because as buyers, we want everything to be focussed on us. We want to feel like the people we are buying from understand our needs, are capable of delivering and are on our side.
Using the term "we" solidifies the relationship between buyer and seller as it portrays a unity and a "team" effort that using the word "I" completely eliminates.

How can you use it?

In early stage sales conversations, using the word "we" is much more effective at establishing a bond and creating unity between you and your potential client. Taking a "team" approach to your client engagements and being "on their side" makes the sales transaction run more smoothly and feels better too. It all starts with "we".

An example

Think of a time when a salesperson has told you how great they are, how great their product is and told you more about them than they have asked about you as the buyer. Now think about the likelihood of you buying - are you more or less connected to that person?
Exactly.

Try this:

Try to use the word "we" more often in your sales conversations to remind the buyer that you will be on their team, fighting with them to solve the issues they face. They don't have to face this alone any more...

See also:

- Communication Basics > The Honesty Effect
- How to Engage > The Empathy Effect

How to Get Attention

Yoo-hoo! Over here! Here I am!

For any sale to take place, you need to seize the attention of your potential buyer in the first place.

With the human attention span sitting at circa 8 seconds, there is a need for boldness and directness to help you stand out, get seen and then move on to hopefully making the sale.

So, what is it that gets attention?

How is it possible to break through the noise and the multitude of things vying for the attention of your buyer?

Let's find out...

Propinquity

- *The more you see me, the more you want to buy me.*

What is it?

Propinquity is "the state of being close to someone or something; proximity." It's the fancy way to describe the fact that the more you see something, the more favourably you feel about it.

Why does it work?

Essentially it comes down to exposure. The more you see something, the more you are exposed to it, the more familiar and favourable it becomes. This is how brands such as Coca Cola or McDonalds work so well, we are familiar with them and what they stand for - so we stick with the devil we know.

How can you use it?

If you want to be noticed, be active in communicating with your prospects. If you can advertise and be on as many social platforms as possible, as often as possible you increase your exposure and thus increase levels of familiarity and loyalty.

More exposure = more chance of business.

An example

You will have "relationships" with brands you have never and will never buy. The advertising we see shapes our thinking and feeling towards brands and we become familiar with them even if we never choose to buy them or need to buy them.

Try this:

Being active on social media every single day can be a very powerful driver of awareness. If you can post valuable (not selling) content that is useful to your potential clients and interesting, and they see it often, then you are nurturing a relationship with them which can make them more likely to buy as they know more about who you are and what you offer.

See also:

- Communication Basics > The Honesty Effect
- How to Get Attention > The Like & Share Effect
- How to Get Attention > The Tagline Effect
- How to Engage > The Empathy Effect

Freemium

- *Create a connection with a free offering and then sell afterwards.*

What is it?

Freemium is where a free sample or free version of a product or service is offered to give you a chance to experience first-hand the value on offer.

Why does it work?

It works because it creates a relationship with the potential client, triggers reciprocity and also Propinquity. Once a client can "taste" how good your offering is, they are more likely to pay for it.

How can you use it?

Creating a forever-free version of your service or offering free samples of physical products are the main methods to engage clients and get them to experience first-hand what you do.
Consider what you can give away for free- much like an aftershave tester or food trial, to attract potential clients.

An example

An example would be the perfume / aftershave testers in shops. You can smell some of the fragrance and then decide if you want to buy it. If you can't smell it, then paying £50 or £100 is a huge gamble.

Try this:

Depending on your offering can you share some of it for free or create a very basic free version of it that will encourage potential buyers to try it? We share free content from our selling confidence course so potential buyers can understand what the course may look like and cover so that they can then make a decision about buying it.

See also:

- How to Engage > Lead Magnet
- How to Convert > The Early Bird Effect
- How to Convert > The First Purchase Effect
- How to Convert > The Free Gift Effect
- How to Convert > The Prize Draw Effect
- How to Convert > The Loss Leader Effect

Censorious

- *Mistkaes can seeze attension'*

What is it?

Censorious people are those who are very critical of others. People with an eye for detail. Pedants. By desirably making mistakes you can catch attention and engage this type of potential client.

Why does it work?

It works using the Von Restorff Effect. Anything incorrect is quite obvious and stands out to Censorious people and thus it will catch their attentions.

How can you use it?

There are 4 ways to do this, but let your creativity run away with how this could integrate with your business:

1. Make an obvious mistake in your sales copy.
2. Promise to attach something to an email but don't.
3. Make any kind of deliberate mistake that is so obvious to spot that potential buyers will know it's deliberrrate.

An example

There is a rumour that Starbucks deliberately spell their clients names incorrectly to garner attention on social media - it certainly does work!

Try this:

Can you make a social media post with a really obvious spelling or grammar mistake to seize attention? Once spotted, the comments will appear and it will drive awareness and engagement with minimal damage to your brand.

See also:

• How to Get Attention > The Von Restorff Effect

Cake Mix Selling

- ***Make it easier for your clients- step by step.***

What is it?

If you've ever bought cake mix, then you will know that on the side of the box are very simple instructions for how to "make" the cake. So easy a child could do it – and that's often the point. The question is, could you reduce your complex offering, instructions, processes and messaging to the complexity level of a box of cake mix?

Why does it work?

It works because of the Path of Least Resistance. You are more likely to engage with and sell to someone as you have done "the work" for them and removed any unnecessary need to think or act- they just need to follow a simple process to buy.

How can you use it?

Think about how you can make dealing with you a piece of cake. How could you make your offering as simple as cake mix? a step by step process? pictures? numbers? The simpler. The better.

An example

There is a popular website in the UK- "We Buy Any Car". Not only does the company name tell you what they do, their tagline is a form of Cake Mix Selling" "Enter your reg number now at webuyanycar.com". This simple message is memorable, explanatory and simple.

Try this:

If you don't already have one, create a step by step process of how you work or how your product works. Illustrate it, perhaps film it, and share it on your website and social media. By giving clients a simple step by step understanding of your offering, you maximise the chances of them understanding and engaging with you.

See also:

- How People Work > The Path of Least Resistance
- How People Work > WYSIWYG
- How to Get Attention > The Show and Tell Effect
- How to Get Attention > The Named Process Effect
- How to Get Attention > The Logic Effect
- How to Get Attention > The Ambiguity Effect

The Before / After Effect

- ***Don't change beliefs, transform the believer.***

What is it?

The Before and After Effect describes the powerful impact that contrasting the before and after of your offering has on your potential client.

Why does it work?

It's a form of Social Proof which helps your potential client to have more confidence in your offering as they are seeing proof that you deliver the results that you say you do and that your potential client wants.

How can you use it?

This works best when there are visual results that can be displayed in the before and after, but this is not always the case.
If what you do lacks this visual element then focussing on the facts and figures, the top line achievements to provide a simple A/B 1/2 contrast can work just as well.

An example

The most common and obvious example here is fitness. Having a picture of someone overweight and then that same person much slimmer (stood next to a life-size cut-out of their former self) is a classic image we can all relate to.

Try this:

If the end result of your offering is visual, then you can simply display a before and after photograph to illustrate the visible difference. If the end result is less tangible then you can use graphs, pie charts or statistics to communicate visually the before and after difference you have created.

See also:

- How People Work > Sell the Destination
- Communication Basics > The Framing Effect
- Communication Basics > Confidence. Certainty. Expertise.
- How to Get Attention > The Show and Tell Effect
- How to Engage > The Law of Inaction

The Humour Effect

- *Laughing all the way to the bank.*

What is it?

The Humour Effect looks at how "humorous" things catch our attention and are more memorable as they stand out.

Why does it work?

The human brain recognises contrast and is sensitive to the unusual. Much like the Von Restorff Effect, The Humour Effect is a tool to be remembered and to capture attention.

How can you use it?

How can you add some comedy and light heartedness to what you do? perhaps use puns or jokes in your marketing, have a light-hearted Twitter feed?
There are a number of potential things you can do, but being humorous for the sake of it isn't always the best approach- proceed with caution.

An example

KFC is an example of this. They follow only a few people with their official twitter account. Six men called Herb and the 5 Spice Girls. This is a non-obvious reference to their 11 Herbs and Spices. It became viral in 2017 and displays a sense of humour and unusual approach to their messaging. See for yourself here - https://twitter.com/kfc/following

Try this:

Is there something funny you can contrast your offering to which is nonsensical but would seize attention?
"This book is the best fly swatter you will buy this year" or a client quote: "I no longer have a wobbly table thanks to buying Understand Your Buyer - highly recommended." Being a little silly and irreverent is a great way to capture attention and engage buyers with your playful side.

See also:

- How to Get Attention > The Bizarreness Effect
- How to Get Attention > The Jingle Effect
- How to Get Attention > The Controversy Effect
- How to Get Attention > The SEX Effect

The Bizarreness Effect

- *Being weird. Works.*

What is it?

The Bizarreness Effect looks at how "bizarre" things catch our attention and are more memorable as they stand out.

Why does it work?

The human brain recognises contrast and is sensitive to the unusual. Much like the Von Restorff Effect, The Bizarreness Effect is a tool to be remembered and to capture attention.

How can you use it?

How can you stand out in your field? Could you offer an ultra-high price version of what you do? or an ultra-budget version? could you adopt a brightly coloured branding style? or a minimalist approach? There are a number of potential things you can do, but standing out for the sake of standing out isn't always the best approach - proceed with caution.

An example

The Bizarreness effect is often seen in advertising. Unique adverts such as "Flat Eric" for Levi's or the Phones4U "Scary Mary" adverts in the UK are examples of using bizarre characters and imagery to seize client attention.

Try this:

One of the simplest ways to stand out visually is to use strong colours. Whether they are bright vibrant colours, or as with this book using Black and White. Bold and contrasting colours make you stand out visually- they can also become part of The Signature Effect which we cover later in the book.

See also:

- How to Get Attention > The Humour Effect
- How to Get Attention > The Von Restorff Effect
- How to Get Attention > The Controversy Effect
- How to Get Attention > The SEX Effect
- How to Get Attention > The Special Edition Effect
- How to Get Attention > The Signature Effect
- How to Get Attention > The Jingle Effect
- How to Engage > The Personification Effect

The Von Restorff Effect

- *Want to stand out? Be* **BOLD**.

What is it?

The Von Restorff Effect looks at the fact that when something stands out in some way, it gets noticed. This is essential for sales messaging as it allows you to engage clients
without them having to read the full content of your email/webpage.

Why does it work?

The human brain naturally looks for contrast. When something stands out in some way- in this case by being highlighted – it is more likely to be noticed and engaged with.

How can you use it?

If you highlight and bold key sections of your emails and web pages, you can be sure to catch people that "skim" the content and draw them in to play closer attention.
If they don't go any further at least you will have made the point you wish to make.

(You will notice throughout our website we use the Von Restorff Effect.)

An example

You will notice in marketing and advertising that key facts and figures are larger, bolder or different colours to the rest of the text. This is The von Restorff Effect in action. We are naturally draw to text which doesn't match its surroundings. (Also the word "BOLD" above will be the first thing you noticed on this page....)

Try this:

Next time you send an email, highlight words in it that are important so that if the recipient skim reads the email, they will get the overall message. This simple trick can get your emails actually read and acted upon; you've made it easier for the recipient to read it (The Path of Least Resistance)

For more email strategies visit: www.emailkit.co.uk

See also:

* How to Get Attention > The Bizarreness Effect
* How to Get Attention > The Special Edition Effect
* How to Get Attention > Censorious

The Repetition Effect

- *Repetition is the mother of learning.*
- *Repetition is the mother of learning.*

What is it?

The Repetition Effect is quite simply repeating things so they are noticed and understood.

Why does it work?

If you want someone to understand your offering and proceed to buy, you need to repeat why they should care about your product / service. As Human Beings, we are simple souls. Making a couple of good points about your argument and repeating them will ensure you breakthrough our 8 second attention span. It's also utilising The Recency Effect where we are more likely to remember the last thing we hear or see.

How can you use it?

By using a "recap" and bullet point lists to repeat the most important points about your products or services, you can ensure the message gets through. Catchy tag lines are a great way to utilise repetition as each time your client recalls the tagline, they are once more repeating why they should care about your offering.

An example

When you see television advertising such as QVC, they run through everything that is offered in the product they are selling, they then recap it, and recap it again and then they tell you the price. Doing this not only crystallises what is being offered, but makes you eager to learn the price.

Try this:

Next time you give a sales presentation or send an email, rather than just recapping the points you are making at the end, ensure you reference and recap the points throughout the presentation. By repeating the things you want to be remembered, they are more likely to be remembered.

See also:

- How People Work > WYSIWYG
- Communication Basics > The Chinese Whisper Effect
- How to Get Attention > The Show and Tell Effect
- How to Get Attention > The Jingle Effect

The Show and Tell Effect

- *Maximise your mediums.*

What is it?

People absorb information in many different ways. Where some like to read information, others like visual representations or videos to help them to understand. It's important to offer your clients every opportunity to engage with you.

Why does it work?

It works because if you don't appeal to a potential client's learning style then they may simply not engage or understand what you are communicating.

How can you use it?

Communicating your message using images, videos and graphics where possible will maximise your chances of engagement. The simplest thing you can do is to use imagery that complements your written messaging and provides visual explanations of the subject matter.

An example

The best example are the videos you see in your Facebook or LinkedIn feed. The ones that you take notice of are the ones with subtitles as most videos are viewed with the sound off. By having both sound and subtitles, those advertisers have made it easier for you to consume their content and increased their chances of seizing your attention.

Try this:

The next time you post on social media, try creating a text, video and visual version of the content. By repurposing the content in multiple ways, you increase your reach and the likelihood of being seen.

See also:

- How People Work > The Path of Least Resistance
- Communication Basics > The Inverted Pyramid
- Communication Basics > Schemas
- How to Get Attention > The Repetition Effect
- How to Get Attention > The Before / After Effect
- How to Get Attention > Cake Mix Selling
- How to Engage > The Repurposing Effect
- How to Engage > The Education Effect

The Respect Effect

- *Manners cost nothing, but can earn you a fortune.*

What is it?

Remembering to be courteous and respectful of everyone you meet is an essential component to making the sale. If you want to sell, you have to be nice. There's no way around it.

Why does it work

It works because if you want to sell to someone, they need to know, like and trust you. How many times have you decided not to buy from a particular place due to a poor past experience that stems from basic rudeness or lack of courtesy? Your clients' emotions trump their logic so it makes sense that you treat everyone as well as you can. Your reputation is a fragile thing and the slightest negative feedback can undo a lot of good work (and cost you the sale).

How can you use it?

Sounds simple, but remembering to be nice and courteous to everyone you meet - prospect, client,

suppliers, will put you in the best position to succeed. If you get angry, riled or lash out then you can damage your reputation and the chances of selling (even if you are "in the right").
Remember: Above all else. Be nice.

An example

Have you ever had a handwritten birthday / Christmas card from a company you have bought from? It's a rare thing indeed, so if you have then this company not only stands out, but they have demonstrated that they care about you and it's not all just about business and money.

Try this:

Next time you give a presentation, have a phone call, or have the buyers sitting in front of you- always begin by thanking them for their time and noting that you appreciate it. Send thank you cards to people that do nice things for you and Christmas cards to clients and acquaintances. Do the right thing, be nice, be polite and not only does it feel good – it makes those people feel good about you and your offering too.

See also:

- How People Work > Emotion Trumps Logic
- How to Engage > The Empathy Effect
- Communications Basics > The Honesty Effect

The Named Process Effect

- *If you name it, you imply value.*

What is it?

If your offering involves a "process" or system then you can add value, credibility and memorability by naming your process. Having a named process not only helps you and your clients to communicate more effectively, it makes something intangible more tangible and thus more valuable.

Why does it work?

It works because we only name things we care about or that have value. Having a named process implies the quality, experience and level of authority that is not present when the process has no name.

How can you use it?

Think about the systems and processes you have in your own business. Could you create a name or acronym that explains the system or process you follow?
The name of the process doesn't have to be related to the nature of your business, but if it can be, it

implies yet more authority and forethought on your behalf.

An example

There are many examples of named processes in daily life, one of the most well-known is the Colonel's Secret Recipe. By calling the recipe for KFC a "Secret Recipe" it implies value and that it's a special thing indeed – not something you will find anywhere else or be able to replicate yourself.

Try this:

If you follow a process to deliver the result for your client, you can give it a name by experimenting with the following, putting your company name, product name or the end result in the name where our see "XXX"

> The XXX Effect
> The XXX process
> The XXX System
> The XXX Plan
> The XXX Equation
> The XXX Method
> The XXX Formula

For more help, visit:
www.howtonamesomething.com

See also:

- Communication Basics > The Chinese Whisper Effect
- Communication Basics > Confidence. Certainty. Expertise.
- How to Get Attention > Cake Mix Selling
- How to Get Attention > The Logic Effect
- How to Get Attention > The Signature Effect

The Personalised Effect

- *An opportunity with your name on it.*

What is it?

We are more likely to buy things that are
personalised with our name on them, or respond to
things that have been personalised for us such as
email.

Why does it work?

It works because we are our own favourite person.
Our name is the most important word in our world
so when we hear or see it, we respond positively.
When a product is personalised, the novelty of a
Coke bottle or a Nutella jar with your name on it
becomes an even more powerful force to move you
to buy.
The "Share a Coke" promotion is also limited which
is utilising The Scarcity Effect.

What can you do about it?

This is a very limited exercise by definition, but
what could you personalise about your offering
that would appeal to your potential buyers?

How could you make your communications more personalised and include the client's name to seize their attention?

An example.

As mentioned, the "Share a Coke" campaign had been highlighted successfully in the UK. Nutella and Famous Grouse Whiskey have similar personalisation to their products for special occasions and Christmas.

Try this:

If you have a physical product offering and if it's appropriate, can you allow your clients to personalise, customise or put their actual name on the product itself?

See also:

- How to Get Attention > The Special Edition Effect
- How to Engage > The Exclusive Effect

The Logic Effect

- *People buy logic.*

What is it?

The Logic Effect looks at the fact that your buyers will process your offering and their needs in a logical fashion – if you change the order you will risk engagement.

Why does it work?

If works because as humans we are logical creatures; we like to do one thing at a time in order to completion. Any deviation from a logical series of events will create a potential barrier to understanding, engagement and thus a barrier to the sale.

The word logic itself comes from how you connect the spoken word in terms of viewpoints and assumptions. Logic is the core factor to keep your potential client's attention and engagement.

How can you use it?

Considering your offering from the client perspective; what are the steps they need to follow to get the best from your offering? How will your offering deliver the value your client needs and is it described in a logical order?

Consider how much information is presented at one time (to avoid Overchoice) and whether it allows for emotional or rational engagement.

An example.

Being logical is one of the cornerstones of creating a C.L.E.A.R Sales Message. The word "CLEAR" itself describes what it takes to be clear – Client focussed, Logical, Engaging, Accurate and Results driven.

Try this:

Draw a line from left to right. On the left is your client at their current point, on the right is the ultimate end result they seek from you. What logical process occurs as they pass from left to right? Can you demonstrate this timeline and logically explain how everything you offer will get them to where they want to be?

See also:

- How to Get Attention > The Named Process Effect
- How to Get Attention > Cake Mix Selling
- How to Get Attention > The Ambiguity Effect
- How to Engage > The Because Effect
- How to Engage > The Scoring Effect

The Controversy Effect

- *Because being rude gets attention.*

What is it?

The Controversy Effect is all about using controversial language and concepts to capture the attention of your potential buyer and make yourself more memorable.

Why does it work?

It works because the brain notices contrast in the environment and unusual things – both visually and verbally. Incorporating controversial language and concepts into your messaging also triggers feelings and memories related to them. This can both capture attention and intrigue - gaining valuable seconds in the battle for client attention.

How can you use it?

Using controversial references are not suitable for everyone. That said, you can harness the benefits of this effect in more subtle ways than you may think. Opposing popular ideas and beliefs that are related to your offering as well as using opinionated and strong language that indicates a stance can both do the trick. Failing that, using language that is on the edge of acceptability such as "slut" can capture attention. (www.egglsut.com)

An example

The Brand Castlemaine XXXX used to use the tagline that their drinkers didn't give a "XXXX" about any other beer. Using their name and suggesting it's a four-letter swearword captured attention - and market share.

Try this:

Can you use the "XXXX" strategy in your messaging but refer to an actual four letter word that isn't offensive? Could you refer to using "The C Word" but that the word is actually "Christmas"? Treading **very** carefully, how could you include some bold and controversial language into your communication.

See also:

- How to Get Attention > The SEX Effect
- How to Get Attention > The Bizarreness Effect
- How to Get Attention > The Humour Effect

The Sex Effect

- *Because sex sells.*

What is it?

The Sex Effect is one of the most commonly used methods of seizing attention in marketing and messaging. At a basic human level, we are constantly assessing our environment - Can I eat it? Can I kill it? Can I have sex with it?

Why does it work?

It works because Sex is a universal draw for attention and interest. Man, woman, gay or straight we all have a biological interest in sex which is triggered by sexual imagery or terminology. The desire to have sex or to make ourselves a more desirable sexual partner drives many of our decisions in everyday life.

How can you use it?

Using sexual references and imagery are not suitable for everyone. That said, you can harness the benefits of this effect in more subtle ways than you may think. How does your offering make your client a more attractive person? Could you show your offering alongside attractive people and places? It doesn't always have to be explicit to work.

An example

Examples of sex in advertising are plentiful. Durex condoms have a current advert about the size of a chilli relative to how hot it is which is a reference to penis size and the well-known phrase "It's what you do with it that counts".

Try this:

If you have a physical product, can you photograph it in a suggestive way that would suggest it's a body part or person rather than your product? Could you describe your process of working in a suggestive way "It's long, hard and painful... but we all need tax accounting".

See also:

- How People Work > Emotion Trumps Logic
- How to Get Attention > The Controversy Effect
- How to Get Attention > The Humour Effect
- How to Get Attention > The Bizarreness Effect

The Ambiguity Effect

- **_Don't make your clients fill in the g_ ps._**

What is it?

The Ambiguity Effect covers the fact that we prefer specific information and knowns to vagueness and unknowns.
Given the choice, we will choose something more specific and defined than not. This is why being a specialist rather than a generalist is a powerful thing in your business.

Why does it work?

It works because we are looking for confidence, certainty and expertise when we buy. If the information or offering appears vague and undefined to us, then it's less attractive. Given the choice we would opt for a "boiler specialist" over a general plumber or an Audi specialist garage over a general garage.
Choosing something more specific and known feels safer to us as we are avoiding the unknown and the "risks" that may follow. For that reason, the Ambiguity Effect is also a form of Zero Risk Bias.

How can you use it?

Ensure that when you are communicating with potential clients, you are being as specific as possible. If you can use numbers, dates, facts or any kind of very specific information you will increase your chances of being noticed and increase your chance of engaging the client to buy.

An example

Our book on writing tag lines is entitled How to Write a Tagline: 74 ready to use templates and ideas. If it was entitled The Tagline Bible or The Tagline Book, then you are less sure of what to expect as it's less specific. This alone could cause you to buy or not - however good the book actually is.
Remember: Specifics sell, generics repel.

Try this:

How could you literally spell out to your clients what you do? Could you have a more descriptive name or website address? Could you really define the result you achieve or return on investment you provide to buyers? Think about stopping a stranger in the street- what would you say to them for them to "get" what you do in just a few seconds?

See also:

- How People Work > The Guessing Game
- How People Work > WYSIWYG
- Communication Basics > The Facts and Figures Effect
- How to Get Attention > Cake Mix Selling
- How to Get Attention > The Logic Effect
- How to Engage > Information Gaps

 # The ICON Effect

- ***A picture paints a thousand words.***

 What is it?

Whilst using words and language to communicate is important, seizing attention is made easier by the use of graphics and icons. The Icon Effect looks at the use of well-known and understood icons- the type you would find on your computer, phone or across the internet - things like padlocks and chat bubbles.

 **Why does it work?**

It works because we already understand certain signs, symbols and icons that are used in everyday life. If you are able to use these in your messaging, you can help to shortcut our understanding of what you offer.

How can you use it?

If appropriate to your offering, you can include common icons in your sales messaging to help seize the attention and understanding of your potential buyers. Using icons in conjunction with sales messaging text can dramatically improve your chances of being noticed and engaging a potential buyer.

 An example

Motorway travel is the best example of this in action. On motorway signs, they need to communicate things quickly and clearly to drivers. You know the icon showing a plane indicates there may be planes overhead for example.

 Try this:

Taking the benefits of your offering, could you create a set of icons that represents the money saving, time saving or other benefits that you bring to your buyers? Having these icons alongside the text increases the chance of engagement.

See also:

- How People Work > The Guessing Game
- How People Work > WYSIWYG
- How to Get Attention > The Logic Effect
- How to Get Attention > The Hashtag Effect

The Christmas Effect

- ***Ho ho ho...... BUY NOW!***

What is it?

The Christmas Effect occurs when you tailor your offering in some way to make it more relevant to the Christmas season.

Why does it work?

It works because at Christmas all we talk about is Christmas. (Starting November and ending promptly at midnight on Christmas Day...)
Even the most pedestrian of products or services can be repackaged in a festive way to garner attention and make the most of the holiday season. The Christmas Effect is in fact The Timely Effect, but as Christmas is such a universally celebrated holiday and so commercially focussed, it deserves to be an Effect in its own right... it is Christmas after all....

How can you use it?

Can you repackage your offering as a gift? Can you align your offering to Christmas itself? Can you add festive decorations to your messaging or social media posts?

Injecting Christmas into any area of your offering can capture interest and help you to ride on the crest of the Christmas wave. By December 26th it will all be over so make hay while the snow shines...

An example

As well as iconic things such as the Coca Cola Truck, Starbucks use Red Cups at Christmas time for a limited period which drives interest and sales - red also encourages buyers to feel differently about their purchase versus a plain white, "cold" cup.

Try this:

You can create a special version of your offering that is geared towards Christmas by changing the colours and imagery you use to advertise it. Incorporate rich reds, greens and purples into your offering to signify a more "Christmassy" feel.

See also:

- Communication Basics > The Timely Effect
- How to Get Attention > The Special Edition Effect
- How to Get Attention > The Events Effect
- How to Convert > The Gift Effect

See also: Psychology of Colour

The colours you use can have an impact on your buyer and drive their engagement and decision making. The best Christmas colours to use are Red, White Silver, Gold, Green

The Price Per Use Effect

- *This book is less than 10p per page!*

What is it?

The Price Per Use Effect is about reframing the price of your offering in the context of what it truly costs your buyer each time they use it.

Why does it work?

It works because it allows you to display a far lower "price point" which can seize attention, it can also allow potential buyers to understand the value of your offering using more relevant real world information than simply the headline price.

How can you use it?

Can you make your pricing model one that can be reframed to a price per use? If per use isn't feasible then you can pick another variable such as time - price per month or if it were a book price per page. The principle here is to get to the lowest number possible to seize attention from potential buyers.

An example

Fuel is the most common, but less obvious example. We buy fuel in litres, but it's often measured in vehicles in gallons (miles per gallon). As a gallon is much more expensive than a litre, the smaller size is used to set the price.

Try this:

Whatever your offering, break it into a smaller price, you can use the following to experiment:

- Per day
- Per week
- Per month
- Per litre
- Per page
- Per minute
- Per hour
- Per use
- Per gram
- Per KG
- Per Mile
- Per Metre
- Per CM
- Per MM
- Per any dimension of space and time...

See also:

- Communication Basics > The Framing Effect
- How to Engage > Equivalence
- How to Engage > Anchoring
- How to Convert > The Comparison Effect

See also: Psychology of Price

The numbers you use "per use" in the price can have an impact on your buyer and drive their engagement and decision making.

- # The Special Edition Effect

- ## *This is the bullet point page edition of the book.*

- ## What is it?

  The Special Edition Effect is all about taking your offering and tailoring it to make it unique and special in some way.

- ## Why does it work?

- It works because as humans we appreciate novelty and find it easier to relate to very specific offerings that appeal to very specific people or needs. Combining brands (as Coke do in the photo) also creates a degree of novelty which also allows the product to stand out by utilising The Bizarreness Effect.

- ## How can you use it?

- Can you create a special version of your offering to appeal to a certain type of buyer?

- Could you create a special version of your offering that appeal to a certain type of need?
- Could you create a special version of your offering that is related to a particular niche in your marketplace?
- Could you co-brand with another company to create a special edition offering?

- **An example**

- There is a lip balm you can buy which tastes like Marmite. It's a special edition created for those who love Marmite and something that will stand out, be noticed and bought by a very specific group of people who both like Marmite and use lip balm.

- **Try this**

- Using the buyer type example, could you create a special version of your offering for a certain type of buyer? Could it be for those who have never done XX or used XX before? Could you create a "beginners" version of your offering for inexperienced clients?

See also:

- How to Get Attention > The Christmas Effect
- How to Get Attention > The Von Restorff Effect
- How to Get Attention > The Bizarreness Effect
- How to Get Attention > The Personalised Effect
- How to Engage > The Exclusive Effect
- How to Engage > The Premium Effect

The Signature Effect

- *Everything we do is Black and White.*

What is it?

The Signature Effect is about making your offering recognisable by creating a "signature" element. Something that is the same throughout all you do.

Why does it work?

It works because as human beings we notice patterns and spot trends. When we see the same words or colours we form a more solidified image in our minds. This means that not only are you more memorable, but that when you create new products or services and include the signature, they will be more recognisable. It's essentially creating your own Schema for your offering.

How can you use it?

Can you include imagery, colours, words or features of your offering that can be the same throughout? The Signature for Clear Sales Message is Black and White. We also produce short, easy to action content so you know that anything new from us will be just as simple to implement. Think about "how" you do what you do and if that can be turned into a recognisable "signature" for your business.

An example

Product (RED) is a charitable product type where major brands produce versions of their product in RED to signify that proceeds from that sale will go to charity.

Try this:

Picking the colour idea in particular, can you incorporate a "signature" colour into all you do? From your logo to your emails to your products to your uniforms?

See also:

- How to Get Attention > The Special Edition Effect
- How to Get Attention > The Bizarreness Effect
- How to Get Attention > The Named Process Effect

The Events Effect

- *An Eventful way to seize attention.*

What is it?

Organising a sale "event" which is relevant to your offering or your buyer can create interest and channel attention.

Why does it work?

It works because it borrows some of the Scarcity Effect to create an event which is time limited. It concentrates attention and perhaps is coupled with a free gift or some sort of additional incentive that drives buyers to take action before the event ends.

How can you use it?

Depending on your offering you can hold an in-person event and have balloons, food and build some real-world atmosphere to invite people to your physical space. Alternatively, you can create an online event which is coupled with something meaningful such as a product launch or important event for your buyers.

An example

Car dealerships are the most common example of the Events Effect in action. Your local car dealership will have "special events" from time to time which are signified by balloons on the forecourt and perhaps some signage. These events might be "VIP" events or to showcase new models, but the point is it gets your attention and catches your eye – aren't you a VIP? Why weren't you invited?

Try this:

Pick a date or an occasion and have a focussed event for your offering. It could be the anniversary of the business, tied to a public event such as Valentine's day or be an invented reason such as "VIP" or "Loyal Customer" event. The reason for the event is only so important, holding the event in the first place and using it to gain attention and new clients is the real focus.

See also:

- Communication Basics > The Timely Effect
- How to Get Attention > The Christmas Effect
- How to Convert > The Scarcity Effect
- How to Convert > The Early Bird Effect

The New Version Effect

- *Continual evolution drives continual sales.*

What is it?

Releasing new versions of your offering provides more opportunities to sell.

Why does it work?

It works because we are all drawn to the latest things - it's Shiny Object Syndrome. By releasing new versions of your product or creating new versions of a service you are refreshing how your clients perceive you, encouraging them to buy more and buy again and as each version develops you may serve your clients in new and more diverse ways.

How can you use it?

Depending on your offering, you can consider updating and releasing new versions on regular intervals such as annually. By making clients aware of your continual improvement it's possible to attract and convert more sales as you regularly have new things to talk about.

An Example

The best example here is the iPhone. From 3 to 4 to 5 to 6 to 7 to 8 to X to XS and XL there have been numerous iterations and changes to the iPhone which only serve to make it more attractive and encourage you to consider upgrading and getting the latest model.

Try this:

The simplest way to keep your offering updating is to tie it to the year. Each year how can you adapt your product or service? How can you add extra features or remove complexity to make it as exciting as the latest iPhone? Each year you can then promote the 2018, 2019, 2020 version of your offering to make it clear that things have changed and improved since the last year.

See also:

- How People Work > Shiny Object Syndrome
- How to Get Attention > The NEW Effect
- How to Convert > The Trade in Effect

The Jingle Effect

- *I'm Lovin it!*

What is it?

A jingle is a catchy noise, tune or song used as an audible logo to make your company / offering more memorable.

Why does it work?

It works because some songs and jingles are created to be deliberately catchy and memorable. You will likely still know some advertising jingles now that you first heard in your childhood.
It mostly works because despite their effectiveness, there are relatively few jingles out there being used. This means that creating a catchy jingle and sharing it is a great way to be remembered by clients.

How can you use it?

If appropriate to your offering, you can create a jingle by first focussing on the main message you want to get across. You can then write lyrics that convey the message using various techniques such as rhyming, alliteration and repetition. The key to creating a successful jingle is something that is short, catchy and makes you think of the offering it relates to.

An example

In the UK, the washing up liquid Fairy has a quite famous jingle that even the mere mention of it here will have it ringing in the ears of those who know it. Search for "Fairy Liquid jingle" on YouTube to hear it for yourself.

Try this:

For your own offering, could you create a tagline or sentence that could be made to rhyme and set to music? Think about the most important part of your offering and make it your core focus.

See also:

- Communication Basics > The Chinese Whisper Effect
- How to Get Attention > The Humour Effect
- How to Get Attention > The Bizarreness Effect
- How to Get Attention > The Repetition Effect
- How to Get Attention > The Tagline Effect

The Hashtag Effect

- ***#a #simple #way #to #get #noticed.***

What is it?

Using Hashtags allows you to curate your social media content and to be found by those with similar interests.

Why does it work?

It works because on the various social media platforms, hashtags have become a de facto standard in how the posts can be organised and accessed. Using the right hashtag can ensure you are found by the relevant audience simply and at no cost.

How can you use it?

Find out more about how to use Hashtags for Twitter, Instagram and Facebook so you can include them next time you post, each platform will have different relevant and dominant hashtags for your offering.

An example

As Hashtags are used to curate and collate social media posts. No-one "owns" a hashtag but they can be dominated by the volume of the content. #metoo is trending as I write this- an online movement regarding women's rights and rape allegations. Those wishing to be included in the conversation append #metoo to their post and join the curation of posts.

Try this:

Although you can't "own" a hashtag you can develop your own hashtags to use with your product or service. The above example of #metoo works well as it's a common language phrase. Thinking about the common language, thoughts, feelings and situations your clients are in; what are positive things they might say when presented with your offering or solution? Using these hashtags can become a supporting element of your brand.

Examples:

#abouttime
#Ilove<productname>
#nomore<problem>
#<offeringname>

See also:

- Communication Basics > Clustering
- Communication Basics > Schemas
- How to Get Attention > The Icon Effect

The Like & Share Effect

- ***Like and share this chapter to win a prize!***

What is it?

Incentivising your followers to like and share your posts on Facebook can dramatically increase your reach.

Why does it work?

It works because liking and sharing a post is a very simple thing to do, so with the incentive of a prize or discount it becomes a no-brainer activity. Once liked and shared the post is visible to more people and some of those people may in turn also like and share which increases reach exponentially.

How can you use it?

This works best on Facebook, so create a Facebook post, decide on an appropriate prize and timescale and post it encouraging your followers to like and share. This activity can be used both as a brand awareness building exercise or to promote a specific product or deal.

An example

Log into your Facebook account now and start scrolling. It won't take too long at all before you come across this type of post that has been liked and shared by someone you know or a 2nd degree connection. Notice what is being offered and how many people have responded in what time frame. Liking and sharing is an art, not a science.

Try this:

Pick a product or service that you want to sell more of. Decide upon an appropriate prize such as that product for free or a generic prize such as an iPad. Post an image of the product or service you want to sell more of along with the instructions to like and share and the timescale.

See also:

- How to Get Attention > Propinquity
- How to Convert > Social Proof
- How to Convert > The Free Gift Effect

The Star Effect

- *More stars. More sales.*

What is it?

Star ratings are a way to demonstrate approval or quality simply and quickly to potential clients.

Why does it work?

It works because we all understand the star rating system. 1 star is lower quality or approval and 5 star is the highest level of quality or approval. There is no other visual system you can use to demonstrate quickly and simply the quality or approval of your offering.

How can you use it?

Star ratings can be used in two ways. Firstly, they can be used to categorise reviews and client feedback to provide a simple way of getting the overall level of satisfaction and happiness. Secondly they can be used to demonstrate to your clients the quality of your offering. This works at the higher end when offering "5 star" service or quality - or even 6 or 7 stars. The principle we understand here is that the number of stars is directly proportionate to what we should expect.

An example

Amazon is the most obvious example of using star ratings. Everything on the site can be reviewed and given a star rating. We rely on these star ratings to help us make our buying decisions.

Try this:

When you ask clients to review your offering, incorporate a 1-5-star rating where 5 stars is the highest ranking. When you have a collection of reviews you can use the average number of stars as a guide for potential new clients. You can use Google Reviews, Trust Pilot or any other similar service to gain access to a star rating system to make this possible.

See also:

- How to Engage > Loss Aversion
- How to Convert > Social Proof
- How to Convert > Zero Risk Bias

The NEW Effect

- *NEW way to get attention, just in, all new and shiny.*

What is it?

The New Effect is about seizing attention for new products and services by focussing on the fact that they are new.

Why does it work?

When something is NEW. It's more attractive. It's really that simple.

How can you use it?

When you launch a new product or service be sure to include the word "NEW" everywhere possible to ensure your potential clients understand that this is the first time it has been offered for sale.

An example

When new things are launched such as Uber, Airbnb or Tesla, there is a natural buzz around them purely because they are new and as yet unfamiliar.

Try this:

The next time you launch something new, ensure you promote the fact that is new through bold messaging and visual "NEW" signs and symbols. What's new is intriguing, but you first need to identify to your potential buyers that it IS new.

See also:

- How People Work > Shiny Object Syndrome
- How to Get Attention > The New Version Effect
- How to Engage > FOMO

See also: Psychology of Colour

The colours you use can have an impact on your buyer and drive their engagement and decision making. The most commonly used colours to use for "New" things are often Red or Green.

The Tagline Effect

- ***Seize attention, engage and explain in just a few words.***

What is it?

The Tagline Effect is about using a tagline to seize attention and to become more memorable in the mind of the consumer.

Why does it work?

It works because as human beings we have an 8-second attention span and the average reading age of a nine-year-old (if in the UK). The need for a short, explanatory and memorable tagline to aide buyers' understanding of your offering cannot be understated. Taglines exist to explain, engage, seize attention and to help your offering become more memorable.

How can you use it?

Taglines are applicable to any kind of offering and can be used alongside logos, as website headers, on business cards or even merchandise and uniforms. If you don't already have a tagline for your offering, then you aren't utilising a simple and very effective means of communicating with your

clients. You can find out more about taglines and how to create them here:
www.howtowriteatagline.com

An example

There are literally millions of taglines out there to use as an example of their power. Whilst having a tagline works, there are only some that stand the test of time such as "Melts in your mouth not in your hand".

Try this:

One of the simplest taglines to create is one where you list the top two/three benefits of your offering separated by full stops:

e.g. Powerful. Affordable. Reliable.

See also:

- How to Get Attention > Propinquity
- How to Get Attention > The Jingle Effect

The Award-Winning Effect

- ***The time to toot your own horn is now...***

What is it?

The Award-Winning Effect is about using the power of awards and accolades to seize and convert buyer attention.

Why does it work?

It works because it harnesses the power of Social Proof. An award is given often by a panel or at least qualified and respected people who are in a position to pass judgement on your offering. Thus, any award – however seemingly obscure – has the power to sway your buyer.

How can you use it?

Whatever your offering there is almost certain to be an award or several different awards available that you can be considered for. Look at competitors and the awards they have won as well as trade magazines to find the most suitable awards. Whilst any award can have a positive impact on the perception of your offering, the awards given by consumers are the most powerful. (Think "best nappies as voted by mums")

An example

The most obvious examples of "award winning" things we buy are wines. There are countless wine awards across a number of different factors that ensure that there are many "award winning" wines out there standing out from their competitors.

Try this:

Find the awards most relevant to your offering through your competitors, trade magazines and professional associations and actively pursue them. It's very rare an award is given out of the blue, often it's about putting yourself "out there".

See also:

- How People Work > Shiny Object Syndrome
- Communication Basics > The Facts and Figures Effect
- How to Engage > Social Proof

The Themed Sale Effect

- ***Giving people a reason to buy.***

What is it?

The Themed Sale Effect occurs when a sales event is justified in some way by a theme - summer/winter/new season/old season/anniversary etc.

Why does it work?

It works for two reasons. Firstly, because arbitrarily discounting can damage the perception of value for the buyer so it allows the seller to "justify" the discount and not be seen to be giving money away for nothing. Secondly, a themed discount often has time limits attached to it, thus harnessing The Scarcity Effect to drive a quicker buying decision.

How can you use it?

Depending on your offering, you can pick any number of "themes" for your sales which include but aren't limited to:

- Winter
- Summer
- End of season
- Start of season
- Mid-season
- Anniversary
- Christmas
- Easter
- Valentine's day
- Black Friday

An example

The most obvious example of an arbitrary themed sale would be "Black Friday". An American sales event that has been adopted across the world and yet one where few if any know the actual meaning behind it?

Try this:

The next time you have a sale, choose a theme that is most relevant to your offering, but also one that provides a short time frame (such as Black Friday which is supposed to be just a day).

See also:

- Communication Basics > The Timely Effect

See also: Psychology of Price

The numbers you use in your sale can have an impact on your buyer and drive their engagement and decision making.

How to Engage

You've got their attention... now what?

Once you have a client's attention there is an immediate need to capitalise on that attention and to engage.

The following effects look at how you can generate engagement and make a connection with your potential client at any stage in the sales conversation.

Engaging potential new clients can be a simple case of speaking in terms that are understood or offering a contextual backstory to your offering. Some of the following effects are obvious and in common use – you will recognise them in the world around you.
Others are less obvious but no less effective at delivering the engagement you need to drive your clients to buy.

Prepare to engage...

Information Gaps

- ***Create intrigue by delaying information.***

What is it?

An information gap is when you are presented with an incomplete piece of information. A great example would be an email title such as "the one thing you MUST do to engage your clients." This title raises your curiosity and encourages you to engage in the email and click it to find out more

Why does it work?

Information gaps exist because the human brain needs to fill in the gaps when it's presented with information. By using incomplete sentences, questions and alluding to information you are placing the onus on your prospect to enquire further and engage to fill in that information gap.

How can you use it?

If you want to get your emails read, your blog posts clicked on, or if you want to encourage a client to engage with you and take an interest, then information gaps are a great method to achieve this.

An example

Most emails and articles utilise Information gaps to draw you in. "The 6 ways you can change your relationship" or "how to save £100 a day on your mortgage" and similar are cryptic headlines designed to allude to information and cause you to act to "close the gap".

Try this:

How can you present your offering in a way that is deliberately intriguing (but not misleading)? For example, this book teaches you how to understand your buyer, but could be described as "80+ secrets, tips and weird techniques to get clients eating out of your hand." By changing the language and using terms such as "secret" or "tip" we can make the information feel more valuable and create further intrigue.

See also:

- How People Work > The Guessing Game
- How to Get Attention > The Ambiguity Effect
- How to Engage > Reactance

Equivalence

- *Comparing something understood to something not yet understood.*

What is it?

Equivalence is when you compare one thing to another in order to develop a greater understanding. If you had a mobile hairdressing company you could request visit you, you might describe it as "the UBER of hairdressing" to allow us to understand how it works.

Why does it work?

It works because it connects the familiar things we know – UBER in this example, with something new – hairdressers that visit us. The greater level of understanding increases the likelihood of engagement with our client, because if they don't understand it they can't buy it.

How can you use it?

If you have a new concept, product or idea, then comparing it's features to something familiar such as UBER will give you an edge when explaining.

Similarly, if you need to explain the cost of something you can provide equivalent examples such as "the same as a cup of coffee per day" to place the price in a new context and encourage the prospect to see the true value you are offering.

An example

The most salient example is "The Rolls Royce of". Using that term implies that whatever the new thing is, it's the best of the best.

Try this:

What qualities does your offering possess that are found in other things? Use the examples below to convey these qualities.

- Quality – Rolls Royce
- Convenience & Speed – Uber
- Customer Service – Virgin
- Innovation- Google

See also:

- Communication Basics > The Framing Effect
- How to Get Attention > The Price Per Use Effect
- How to Engage > Anchoring
- How to Convert > The Comparison Effect
- How to Convert > The Price Match Effect

Anchoring

- **_The first piece of information sets
our expectation._**

What is it?

The first piece of information we read is often our
reference point and becomes an "anchor" for us.

Why does it work?

It works because it provides an opportunity to
structure how a client understands the information
you present. If the first piece of information is a
high price and then you are offered a low price, the
lower price seems more reasonable as it's been
presented in more context.

How can you use it?

Anchoring is often used in pricing. If you have a £5
product and a £50 product, by presenting the £50
product first and then the £5 product, the lesser
priced product feels much better value. Similarly, if
you have a £5, £25 and £50 product, presenting
the £5 first and then the other prices, will make
them feel "more expensive" as your anchor point
was set at £5.

An example

When you see cars advertised on TV and in magazines, notice the small print. The car shown nearly always has higher priced extras and is the best model in the range. In doing this, the car companies anchor you to the sporty looks and great specification of the top of the range model which means anything less is a compromise- this can cause you to upgrade and spend more just to realise the vision of the model you first saw.

Try this:

The next time you present your offering, lead with the highest price possible to anchor the client to the more expensive price. The reality is they will buy the cheaper version, but they will now view this as a much better deal than if you hadn't anchored them to a higher priced offering.

See also:

- How to Get Attention > Price Per Use Effect
- How to Engage > Equivalence
- How to Convert > The Comparison Effect

See also: Psychology of Price

The numbers you use when you anchor can have an impact on your buyer and drive their engagement and decision making.

Loss Aversion

- *Playing to lose instead of playing to win.*

What is it?

Loss Aversion is the phenomena whereby we are more motivated by protecting against losses than seeking gains.

Why does it work?

If we place more weight behind protecting what we have, minimising issues and pain, then as sellers we can focus on these areas to better appeal to prospects.

How can you use it?

Tailoring your sales messaging towards protection, safety and continuity more so than gains and growth can help to close more sales and engage clients as you are connecting with their main drivers.

An example

An obvious example would be life assurance. Leaving your loved ones behind with no money and funeral costs is the common theme in how they message their offering. You buy life assurance not for personal gain - you will literally be dead and never see the money – but to avoid the terrible situation of letting your loved ones down.

Try this:

Consider the cost of inaction your client will face if they don't buy your offering. Paint the picture of just how bad that may be for them and then contrast that with what your offering provides. By detailing the loss and providing a means to avoid it, you are more likely to engage them to buy.

See also:

- How People Work > Emotion Trumps Logic
- How to Get Attention > The Star Effect
- How to Engage > FOMO
- How to Engage > Trigger Point
- How to Engage > The User Generated Content Effect
- How to Convert > Zero Risk Bias
- How to Convert > The Scarcity Effect
- How to Convert> The Pay on Results Effect

First Person Questions

- *Speaking your client's language.*

What is it?

First Person Questions is the art of providing information as the answer to questions that your reader or potential client may have asked in their own language and from their own point of view.

Why does it work?

If you were presented with two links - one was "pricing" and the other was "how much does this cost?", which one do you feel more connected to? Which one are you more likely to click? As humans, we are self-focused and respond positively to things that are in our self-interest. It works because it literally "speaks our language".

How can you use it?

Use plain English terminology to present and link to information. What are the common questions fears and drivers of your potential clients? how can you adapt your content to appeal and how can you phrase questions that would be naturally asked such as "how much does it cost?"

An example

You will notice that the titles on this very page are written in the first person. Rather than explaining each way to understand your buyer by name, we use the convention "what is it?" and "Why does it work?" as this is precisely what you will be thinking. The book is designed to cut straight to the point, be actionable and instantly understood - First Person Questions are our secret weapon to achieve that.

Try this:

For any kind of written communication you make to your potential buyers, consider what they will be thinking, feeling or asking. Shape your messaging to that language as closely as you can and you will find more engagement as your messaging resonates with the client's needs hopes and desires.

See also:

- How People Work > The False Consensus Effect
- Communication Basics > The Chinese Whisper Effect
- Communication Basics > Confidence. Certainty. Expertise.

Reactance

- ***Don't push the red button...***

What is it?

Reactance is the sophisticated name for "reverse psychology" the art of telling people what they can't do and then encouraging them to do it.

Why does it work?

As humans, we are naturally protective of our freedoms. When a freedom is restricted through a challenge such as "don't press the red button" we feel the urge to not only protect our freedom from this blocker, but to immediately exercise our freedom to prove we are in control.

How can you use it?

Reactance is used in sales copy and advertising, often satirically, to move clients to act. For example, I have written a lot more on reactance and can prove it works if you visit here:

http://www.clearsalesmessage.com/reactance-example/

But please don't visit that page

An example

The above is a real-world example of reactance in action - how tempted are you to visit that page? What on earth could be there? What are you missing out on? We'll never know as you won't visit the page.... right?

Try this:

The next time you send an email, make the title "DO NOT OPEN THIS EMAIL". You will almost certainly experience the highest open rate of any email you have sent - I had a nearly 90% open rate when I tried it on my list.
Nothing else was known to the recipient about the email other than the fact they shouldn't open it. Naughty people!

See also:

- How to Engage > Information Gaps

Lead Magnet

- *Offering something of value in exchange for an email address.*

What is it?

A lead magnet is something of value - usually a free pdf or eBook – that is offered to entice someone to sign up to your email list.

Why does it work?

Using the principles of information gaps as well as the Freemium model, lead magnets allow you to engage with new potential clients by giving them something of value, demonstrating your offering and beginning a relationship with them.

How can you use it?

"How to" guides, eBooks, numbered lists, free worksheets and more can be used as lead magnets. As long as what is offered would be of genuine value to the recipient then it's a viable magnet to use.

An example

We use a much shorter version of this book as a Lead Magnet at www.clearsalesmessage.com.

Those that download the pdf join our mailing list and receive our weekly sales tip emails as a result.

Try this:

What information could package as a pdf you share with potential clients for free? Is there a common problem or need they face that you could help them with that would encourage them to buy from you by demonstrating your expertise in this area?

See also:

- How to Get Attention > Freemium
- How to Engage > The Law of Reciprocity
- How to Convert > The Prize Draw Effect
- How to Convert > The Free Gift Effect

FOMO

- ***Fear of Missing Out.***

What is it?

FOMO is the Fear of Missing Out. It's the thought that others around us may have access to information, experiences or resources that we don't.

Why does it work?

It works because it appeals to nearly all of the four basic drivers. We don't want to miss opportunities to learn, grow, connect, prosper and so when that happens - or when we feel that has happened - we experience FOMO which then spurs us to act.
This is why you check your phone and email 100+ times a day. The thought of "missing out" on a new email or status update as it comes in is enough motivation to keep us checking continually when it's a waste of time.

How can you use it?

In the world of sales, the most basic form of FOMO is to describe people that have benefited from your product or service and "alienate" the person

reading the article as they aren't the same.
If you can be really specific and create an
information gap, then FOMO becomes even more
intense.
That's why the 27 people that downloaded this
eBook (http://www.clearsalesmessage.com/1000-
ebook/) now make that extra £1k per month.

An example.

If you didn't click the link above to find out how
those people make extra money each month, then
you will be curious about it and want to know
more. If it is as simple as I make it look then why
wouldn't you check it out- you've got nothing to
lose and you might be missing a trick here…

Try this:

If you want your clients to experience FOMO then
talk about the clients you currently have and the
results they get. By describing the end result the
client seeks and referring to real world people and
companies that benefit from your offering, your
potential buyer can feel left out and driven to
engage.

See also:

- How People Work > Emotion Trumps Logic
- How to Get Attention > The NEW Effect
- How to Engage > Loss Aversion
- How to Engage > The Law of Inaction
- How to Engage > The Scoring Effect

- How to Convert > The Scarcity Effect
- How to Convert > Zero Risk Bias
- How to Convert > The Qualify Effect

The Security Effect

- *At the end of the day, our goals are safety and security.*

What is it?

The Security Effect is where you can use fear of the unknown to drive clients to buy or engage.

Why does it work?

It works because one of the four main human drivers is that of defending. As primitive beings one of our most vital motivators is that of staying alive and staying safe. By bringing attention to safety, or the lack of, you can trigger this driver.

How can you use it?

If there is a negative downside to not using your product or service, then by alluding to this or asking questions about how a client will "deal with that situation when it arises" can shift focus to safety and security and drive the client towards purchasing.
After all, if you don't take that insurance policy or fit those locks then how would you deal with losing all of your possessions if you were burgled?

An example

If you've ever bought a new sofa, you will know that the first thing they try to "upsell" you to is upholstery protection and/or cleaning. What would happen if you don't protect the sofa and spill wine on it? What happens if your kids scribble pen all over it?

Try this:

In your own communication, include some "what if" scenarios to encourage the buyer to consider the alternatives to not buying your offering. What are the unknowns, risks and grey areas and how does your offering protect against or eliminate them?

See also:

- How to Engage > FOMO
- How to Engage > Loss Aversion
- How to Convert > Zero Risk Bias

See also: Psychology of Colour

The colours you use can have an impact on your buyer and drive their engagement and decision making. The most commonly used colours to use for "security" are often blue.

The Generation Effect

- *We prefer the things we create ourselves.*

What is it?

The Generation Effect looks at how we think more favourable about things we have created or are personally "invested in".

Why does it work?

It works because as humans we favour ourselves and what we create in our lives. By tapping into this natural preference for things we have created we can engage our clients by speaking their language.

How can you use it?

Ask your clients what success would look like to them. Get your clients involved in designing products and services, encourage your clients to invest themselves in what you offer and they will be more favourable towards it.

An example

The start of film adverts nearly always begins in the same way "Imagine a world where...."
You are actively being invited to use your imagination and to paint a mental picture of what the film will be like. Yes, you will be shown visuals in the trailer, but by imagining yourself you create your own version of the film and thus connect with it in a different way.

Try this:

Ask your clients to picture their future. Whatever your offering may be, your client will have an image in their mind of what they want it to look like and what will happen. Actively encourage clients to paint that picture and connect with it – they will be more engaged as a result.

See also:

- How People Work > Emotion Trumps Logic
- How People Work > The Curse of Knowledge

The Law of Reciprocity

- *To get, you must first give.*

What is it?

The Law of Reciprocity relates to how we respond positively to reciprocate behaviour. If someone does something for you, you naturally feel inclined to return the favour.

Why does it work?

It works because this is how human nature works. We naturally feel the need to reciprocate both positive and negative behaviour.
We respond to the environment around us often by mirroring the behaviour and energy we receive.

How can you use it?

In a sales context, The Law of Reciprocity is ideal when sharing information or providing free samples or examples of your offering. By providing something of value for free, your prospect is more likely to want to reciprocate and move towards buying your product. Certainly more so than if you tried to "sell" to them without providing any value for free to begin with.

An example

Google is a fine example here. They share the most powerful and efficient search tools on the web with you for free and in return you build an image of trust and confidence in Google. When they try to sell you something you are more inclined to make the purchase because not only do you trust them and have a relationship with them, you have also benefited from them "for free" and naturally feel inclined to repay the favour.

Try this:

Depending on your offering, if you can provide advice and some free resources to help them, then that client will be more inclined to buy from you if and when the time comes.

If you want to know what you deserve and how to deserve things, then check out www.youdeservethisbook.com

See also:

- How to Engage > The Good Cause Effect
- How to Convert > The First Purchase Effect
- How to Convert > The Free Gift Effect

The Bystander Effect

- *A group of people diminishes your feelings of responsibility.*

What is it?

When unidentified and in crowds, people feel diminished responsibility and are less likely to act.

Why does it work?

It works because in "anonymity" there is no accountability so we can be as lazy and irresponsible and there are no consequences. This is how you can see people being attacked in the street and no-one does anything. These people are not "responsible" and are expecting others to act - and of course then nothing happens.

How can you use it?

To overcome The Bystander Effect, you need to identify your audience. Use their name, call them out in emails and all communications where possible. Personalise everything you can so that the person feels identified and not anonymous - then they are more likely to act.

This is why marketing emails and letters, coke bottles, cups of coffee and much more features your name - these companies are engaging with you by not allowing you to be anonymous in the crowd.

An example

Most emails and post we get from companies these days is addressed to us and uses our name liberally throughout. Your social media profiles will proclaim "Welcome back James" and emails from supermarkets remind me "James don't forget to stock up for Christmas". Your name is the most important word in the world to you - and savvy marketers know it.

Try this:

If you don't already, use your client's name at every turn possible. On calls, in emails and on your website if you can get your tech people to do the necessary work.
By personalising your approach and singling out a person they are more likely to act and take personality - they can't hide in the crowd as a bystander.

See also:

- How to Engage > The Bandwagon Effect
- How to Convert > Social Proof

The Common Enemy Effect

- *Hatred has the power to unite.*

What is it?

When two sides both "hate" the same thing, they share a "common enemy" despite any other differences they may have.

Why does it work?

It works because sharing anything - but particularly an enemy – bonds us. Having something in common doesn't always have to be a positive thing - we might not like the same things, but if we hate the same things it can bring us together.

How can you use it?

Whatever problem your product or service solves, make THAT problem your "common enemy". Talk negatively about it and focus on its elimination to increase engagement.
How can you show your client you share their enemy and want to support them in waging war against it?

An example

A good friend of mine is a wine supplier. Her
approach is "Life is too short to drink bad wine."
She has made bad wine the common enemy and
dedicates her life and business to supplying and
drinking only the finest wines money can buy. If
you've ever been disappointed by a poor wine (not
all poor wine is cheap) then you will know the
importance of combatting "bad wine".

Try this:

Your offering exists to meet a need or solve a
problem. In your messaging experiment with
making that need or problem your common enemy.
Take sides with your client as to how unfair the
world is and how you are dedicated to helping
them overcome XYZ problem.

See also:

- How People Work > Confirmation Bias
- How People Work > The Law of Past Experience
- How to Engage > The Empathy Effect
- How to Engage > The Good Cause Effect

The Empathy Effect

- *Understanding creates trust.*

What is it?

The Empathy Effect states that we feel more connected to those who understand our situation.

Why does it work?

It works because we feel connected to those who seem to understand and empathise with our situation. That being the case if as the seller you can demonstrate that you understand and empathise with your buyer, you are likely to trigger this connection and thus increase your chances of making the sale.

How can you use it?

Recognise the needs, problems and circumstances of your buyers. Identify and communicate about their feelings, hopes, dreams and fears to demonstrate your level of understanding and empathy.

An example

Adverts for parenting products use empathy well. "We know you want the best for your child, that's why we do XXX" They tap into the emotional motivations that parents experience.

Try this:

Think about the buyers of your offering. What does it look, sound, taste and feel like to face the problems they do? Refer to the circumstances of your client in your messaging and you demonstrate understanding which generates engagement.

See also:

- How People Work > Emotion Trumps Logic
- How People Work > The Treat Effect
- Communication Basics > The Honesty Effect
- Communication Basics > The I/We Effect
- How to Get Attention > Propinquity
- How to Get Attention > The Respect Effect
- How to Engage > The Common Enemy Effect
- How to Engage > The Story Effect
- How to Engage > The Personification Effect
- How to Convert > The Freedom Effect

The Story Effect

- *As humans, we communicate through stories.*

What is it?

The Story Effect states that we connect and communicate primarily through stories.

Why does it work?

As humans, we naturally communicate through the power of stories and storytelling.

How can you use it?

There are two approaches you can apply. Firstly, you can use real world examples of your story or the stories of your clients and those that have had success with your product or service. Secondly, you can create "stories" to explain your product or service in context to better explain how it works and who it's suitable for.

An example

In America, the story of Jared and Subway is well known. Jared wanted to lose weight so ate only

Subway sandwiches and it all worked out well. As a result, potential Subway clients connect Subway to health and weight loss using the real-world story of a real-world person - Jared.

Try this:

If relevant, talk about the story of your company or your offering. How did it come to be? Why does it exist? How has it changed along the way? Being more contextual about your offering can help you connect with clients as they understand your business and offering better as well as viewing you in a more humanistic way than as a "corporate".

See also:

- Communication Basics > The Framing Effect
- How to Engage > The Empathy Effect

The Exclusive Effect

- *If we feel special, we are more likely to buy.*

What is it?

The Exclusive Effect states that we behave differently when we have access to exclusive resources that others don't.

Why does it work?

The literal opposite to FOMO, The Exclusive Effect makes clients feel good when they feel they have exclusive access to things that other people don't have.

How can you use it?

Reward your loyal clients and offer limited and exclusive benefits to new clients to give them the feeling of being special and having advantages over others.

An example

At Ferrari, when a new model launches you can't buy it. You have to be selected to buy it and there are some criteria they follow to allow the most important Ferrari clients first pickings on the latest model.

Try this:

What part of your offering could be made exclusive? Could you allow clients special online access to something, send them something exclusive in the post or hold an event? Events in particular are a great experiential way to show your clients you appreciate them and to make them feel special.

See also:

- How to Get Attention > The Special Edition Effect
- How to Get Attention > The Personalised Effect
- How to Engage > The Business User Effect
- How to Convert > The With-Purchase Effect

The Should Effect

- *Some advice to help conversion.*

What is it?

The Should Effect principally involves telling your client what they "should" or "shouldn't" be doing in their current situation.

Why does it work?

If works because as providers of products and services, we are deemed to be knowledgeable authority figures. If you are advised you "should" or "shouldn't" be doing something from a person of authority, then you are more likely to take heed.

How can you use it?

By confronting your clients with the ongoing effects of both action and inaction in their current situation, you can get them to understand and engage with your offering. Once a client understands why they should or shouldn't do something, they are more likely to buy and if they don't buy then the nagging feeling that they have gone against the advice of an authority figure may cause them to reconsider at a later stage.

An example

Rather than using the word "should" you will find many "serving suggestions" on the sides of food packets which show how you should be consuming their products.

Try this:

Your clients have something they are trying to achieve or a problem they are trying to solve. Using the word "should" or "recommend" in your messaging and conversation implies direction as your experience and credibility in your field means that when you tell someone to do something they should do it as it will work.

See also:

- How People Work > The Authority Effect
- How to Convert > Social Proof
- How to Convert > The Gift Effect

The Anticipation Effect

- *Get excited........ this really works!*

What is it?

The Anticipation Effect is the act of making your clients excited about your products or services by getting them to focus on just how great the end result will be.

Why does it work?

If works because as clients we focus on the end result - "what's in it for us?". The Anticipation Effect recognises this by vividly painting a picture of the future and how it will look and feel to achieve the XYZ thing that your client wants to achieve.

How can you use it?

Remembering to "sell the destination, not the journey" is one of the most powerful things to remember when selling. In early stage sales conversations, you can ask questions like "so what would the perfect outcome look like?" or "how will we know we have succeeded?" to get the client to paint a picture themselves and begin to get excited about achieving their objectives.

An example

When Apple launch new products, they hold a very large event for the media and they are always documented in the world press. Rumours of the events are "accidentally" leaked to the press to build buzz and anticipation so that when the time comes, we are all curious as to what the new products are- and when we can buy them.

Try this:

If you have a product launch, event or other notable thing happening then spend longer than you would normally in building anticipation. Can you tease with information and details or use countdowns and timers to add urgency and anticipation to the equation?

See also:

- How People Work > Sell the Destination
- Communication Basics > The Inverted Pyramid

The Because Effect

- *Because "doing the thinking" helps your buyer.*

What is it?

The Because Effect is an adaptation of The Path of Least Resistance. In this case, we are "doing the thinking" for the client.

Why does it work?

It works because when a client is presented with reasoning for why they should buy a product or service, they are likely to use and favour this argument as the "thinking" has been done for them.

How can you use it?

The Because Effect works very well in FAQ or objection handling scenarios. By presenting the case "because" you can counter objections before they occur. That's why we suggest using this method in your copy – because it can open and close client objections in a single sentence.

An example

Adverts for health and medical products are always "doing the thinking" for us and explaining why certain bacteria do certain things and how we can all look younger by taking XYZ pills because they contain ABC ingredients.

Try this:

This is about causality and logic. In your offering, can you better explain why and how it works and demonstrate that in a simple and logical way that anyone could understand?

See also:

- How People Work > The Authority Effect
- How to Get Attention > The Named Process Effect
- How to Get Attention > The Logic Effect
- How to Convert > Social Proof

The Good Cause Effect

- ***Doing good does great things for your conversion.***

What is it?

The Good Cause Effect is where you ensure that the sale of your products and services does some good in the world.

Why does it work?

It works because as consumers we are all becoming socially more conscious about the world and our impact upon it. If we know that buying X product gives something back, and buying the next competitor doesn't, it can be a deciding factor to making the sale.

How can you use it?

Donating to, affiliating with or supporting a charity that has some degree of relevance will allow you to not only engage with buyers and demonstrate that you give back, but may get you additional exposure through the charity itself and any charitable things you may do to raise funds.

An example

The most famous example of this is TOMS shoes. For every pair of shoes they sell, they provide a pair of shoes to someone in need. Your offering could match a purchase in this way, could donate money to charity or could provide something else such as meals in Africa. The relevance of the good cause offering itself isn't that important, it's the fact that you do some good in the world that will help be a "closing factor" to a potential client.

Try this:

Find a charity that is appropriate and relevant to your offering. Offer to partner, sponsor, donate or affiliate with them.

See also:

- How to Engage > The Law of Reciprocity
- How to Engage > The Common Enemy Effect

The Law of Inaction

- *Inaction is a form of action.*

What is it?

The Law of Inaction describes the fact that even when you take no action or make no choice, you are in fact taking an action and making a choice – EVERYTHING has a consequence.

Why does it work?

It works because you can highlight the cost of inaction to your potential clients and make them aware of the "hidden choices" they are making by choosing to do nothing.

How can you use it?

Contextually in sales copy and conversation, it might look like this:

> *"Not becoming a member and going to the gym is fine and it's your choice, but by choosing to not pursue health and weight loss you are choosing to be less healthy and to potentially put on weight - are you sure that's what you want?"*

An example

Welcome to the exciting world of descaling products. Descaling products use the Before and After Effect to show you how their product works to remove lime scale and to highlight what happens if you don't use their product.

Try this:

In conversation or in your messaging try highlighting the repercussions of the buyer not taking action to resolve this issue or meet their need. They can use any product or service to meet that need, so this isn't about convincing someone to choose you; but the buyer needs to be clear that inaction has consequences and are they prepared for those consequences?

See also:

- How to Get Attention > The Before /After Effect
- How to Engage > FOMO

The "I have a Dream" Effect

- *People like to follow a leader or larger vision.*

What is it?

Using Martin Luther King as our example (classic equivalence) we're talking about products, services and businesses that have a larger vision, stand for something or in some way "have a dream". You can attract, engage and convert clients who share the same vision and values as you if you make clear what your vision and values are.

Why does it work?

It works because it goes beyond "making the sale" and connects with your buyers on a different level. We know that Apple computers are more expensive, but we know they "believe" in a simple user interface that just works and so we're happy to pay more knowing what we will get.
Buying something for a greater reason, a context or a strong "because" can change everything. Think about TOMS shoes who donate a pair of shoes to charity each time they sell a pair. TOMS have a vision to help those worse of and supply shoes to them. It's something that the people working at

TOMS believe in and you can too.

How can you use it?

Having a clear vision or mission and communicating that to clients in all that you do can create engagement. Can you create a "promise" or share your values on your website and throughout your offering so everyone knows what you stand for?

An example

Elon Musk is one of the best examples of a modern-day visionary. From Tesla to Space X to SolarCity, many people buy his products and buy into him because of his large-scale vision and ambition.

Try this:

Do you have a goal, a mission or a belief? If you do, then make this vision clear to your staff and clients alike. Be clear on your mission, the larger context of what you are trying to achieve and what you passionately believe in.
Remember- this is about more than just making the sale.

See also:

- How to Engage > The "People Like You" Effect
- How to Engage > The Identity Effect
- How to Engage > The ECO Effect

The "People Like You" Effect

- *We are attracted to people like us.*

What is it?

Communicating with a "type" of person that uses your products and services in a way that identifies them either through their behaviour, motivations, pains or thinking. This might be "fashionistas" or "fisherman" – it will be a type and group of potential client with identifiable characteristics.

Why does it work?

An extension of The Empathy Effect, the "People Like You Effect" demonstrates your knowledge and understanding of a certain client type through your communication to them.
Your knowledge and anticipation of their needs and situation creates a connection and an impression of confidence and control. This is the one time in sales messaging where jargon and industry/insider terminology is welcomed.

How can you use it?

To identify potential client types in your communication you can use phrases like:

- If you've ever thought XX then you need to do / think/ say XX.
- Have you ever had this problem? We work with people like you.
- We work with people who....

So, for fisherman that might look like this:

- If you've ever thought Fishing is underrated, then you are not alone.
- Have you ever run out of XC-2 bait hooks? We supply replacement and repairs for this baiting system.
- We work with people who know that fishing isn't about the fish - it's about getting away from the world and being in nature.

Those are obscure examples, but the goal is to be obscure and to get the reader to identify with the messaging and be "singled out" as the ideal person that you need to communicate with.

Try this:

Identify the "types" of people who buy from you and then focus on one characteristic in your messaging.
This could be as simple as "for people who put the jam on first" which alludes to a popular British debate about scones or "we like people who like dogs" to align yourself with other dog lovers.
Find one real world characteristic or similarity and focus on it in your messaging to find "people like you".

See also:

- How to Engage > The "I have a Dream" Effect
- How to Engage > The Identity Effect

The Premium Effect

- *Aspirational items are more attractive to buyers.*

What is it?

Having a higher priced version of your offering can make the lesser priced versions seem better value and of a higher quality by association. Whilst not many will purchase your premium offering, a premium offering can drive sales at the lower end of your offering.

Why does it work?

It works because it anchors your potential buyers to a much higher price point which makes the lesser offering seem like a great deal.

If you thought a wheelbarrow was perhaps £20 and found a supplier who has a top of the range £150 wheel barrow and an "entry level" £45 wheelbarrow, then you are happier to buy the £45 version despite it being double your expectation as it's so much "cheaper" than the £150 version.

It also implies a higher level of quality. If the seller offers a £150 version of their product, then surely some of the quality of that makes its way into the £45 product?

How can you use it?

Considering your current offering, could you create an all-out maximum value and maximum price high end version that includes everything?
How could you create a higher value offering that will deliver on the value as well as help to raise the price expectation for your entry level items?

An example

Cars have entry level models and premium models. It's often the premium models that feature in the advertising and it's often the entry level model that you can afford and buy. If the entry level was featured predominantly in the marketing, then would you be as keen to buy the car? Perhaps not...?

Try this:

Can you create a premium (or entry level) version of your offering to appeal to a different type of buyer and allow for upsell and down sell?

See also:

- How People Work > The Law of Past Experience
- How to Get Attention > The Special Edition Effect
- How to Convert > The Mega Pack Effect
- How to Convert > The Buy More Effect

See also: Psychology of Colour

The colours you use can have an impact on your buyer and drive their engagement and decision making. The most commonly used colours to use for "Premium" things are Black, Silver, White and Gold.

The Identity Effect

- *We like to adopt an identity and be part of a wider group.*

What is it?

The Identity Effect looks at grouping buyers together and naming them as a means of creating an identity such as "Beliebers" or "Swifties".

Why does it work?

If works because as humans we seek to align ourselves to a group (or tribe). If we share a love for Justin Bieber and can recognise others who do so it creates a community and sense of cohesion that simply wouldn't exist if there was no name for it.

This is the power of naming things. We only name things of value and significance so if there is a term for your buyers or fans to use then it not only provides the tribal element, it also implies great value and significance.
Having a name for your buyers and fans is a form of branding. When you think of GAP or NIKE or Apple you feel and think certain things. The same is true here - aligning your identity to being a

"KatyCat" is no different to being a "MAC" person instead of a "P.C" person.

How can you use it?

Identities are used for fans of popstars in the main, it's not something that can be applied to every business, but it's something to experiment with. Think about the end result you offer, the positive emotions and feelings you achieve and the name of your business. You can use this list for inspiration. As for people that follow Clear Sales Message? I think we'll call them *"Messengers "*.

Try this:

This is very much dependant on your offering, but if appropriate can you give a name to the types of people who buy from you? Are they "DIYers" or "fitness fanatics"? Perhaps they are "golf widows" or "workaholics". Whichever term you choose, pick one that will have positive connotations

See also:

- How to Engage > The "People Like You" Effect
- How to Engage > The "I have a Dream" Effect
- How to Engage > The ECO Effect

The Patriotic Effect

- *Keeping it country.*

What is it?

The Patriotic Effect focuses on the loyalty we all
feel towards the countries from which we hail and
the countries within which we live.

Why does it work?

It works because at a basic human level, we seek
to support our communities and those around us.
Even in our capitalistic world where price is
paramount, factors such as the country of origin of
a product can be a deciding factor in making the
sale.

How can you use it?

This works for physical products more so than
services and the intangible. If your products are
created in the same country where your business
operates and where your clients are, then you may
find benefit in publicising this fact.
An example.

Vauxhall have been producing cars in the UK for a very long time and they are very keen to point this out in all of their messaging. If you are looking to buy a car and Vauxhall is on the list of possibles – the fact that it was made in the UK (my home country) could be a deciding factor.

Try this:

Include references to your country or the country of origin for your offering in your marketing and messaging. Measure social media engagement on posts mentioning origins to gauge if patriotism matters to your buyers.

See also:

- How People Work > The Local Effect

The Language Effect

- *Speaking your client's language.*

What is it?

The Language effect addresses one simple truth. People buy in their native language more often than not.

Why does it work?

It works because as buyers we are seeking confidence, certainty and expertise. We are seeking a solution to our problems and something to meet our needs that we fully understand.
It's for this reason that we are more likely to buy in our native language and it's for this reason that you need to ensure your offering caters to the native languages of your potential buyers.

How can you use it?

Many businesses operate in English only. This is both a shame and a great opportunity. If you can translate your website, your literature, your offering to the most relevant language(s) to your audience you not only increase your chance of conversion, but you open yourself to a larger pool of potential clients.

An example

The major brands are the example here- Facebook, Google, Coca Cola et al have all created native messaging and sales materials for the different territories within which they operate - it sure works for them.

Try this:

Do some investigation to determine the 2nd most popular language spoken by your buyers after English. Experiment with messaging, websites and adverts in this new language and measure engagement.

See also:

- How People Work > The Path of Least Resistance

The Bandwagon Effect

- *Well, if everyone else is doing it....*

What is it?

The Bandwagon Effect refers to the likelihood of your clients to "follow the crowd" and buy your offering if they see lots of other people have too.

Why does it work?

It works because we are seeking to minimise risk when we buy. If lots of people have seemingly bought your offering and approve of it in reviews and case studies, then as a buyer I am more likely to buy as I feel safer. It's the reason you join queues without knowing what they are for or buy bestselling books on Amazon without doing any research – if it's good enough for the crowds....

How can you use it?

If you can publicise how many people use your product or service and the number is compelling, then it can be used to attract more buyers. Making statements such as "Trusted by over 1,000 businesses" or "Join our mailing list of 15,000 people" it's more compelling than if those numbers were absent.

If appropriate, focus on the scale and reach of your business and promote the large numbers that show your offering is popular and well received.

An example

Mailing lists online will often tell you how many billions of subscribers they have which is using the power of that many people to drive your decision. If that many people have signed up, then surely something is going on....?

Try this:

Find out how much of your offering has been sold to how many people since you began. If the number is large enough you can use this in your messaging – "25,000 people can't be wrong!" The larger the number of people the better - we are trying to demonstrate that your potential buyers should also "jump on the bandwagon".

See also:

- How to Engage > The Bystander Effect
- How to Convert > Social Proof

The Repurposing Effect

- *Yes...you CAN have cereal for dinner.*

What is it?

The Repurposing Effect is the process
of encouraging clients to consume your offering in
new ways.

Why does it work?

It works because sometimes we need to be told
that we can use products and services in new
ways. (An example of WYSIWYG).
Who knew cereal could be a great snack or that
you can use Coca Cola to clean your toilet (True
story). Often when a product or service is
repurposed it can lead to feelings
of exclusivity amongst buyers and create a sub
culture of clients – as evidenced by the cereal cafes
that have popped up across the world.

How can you use it?

If appropriate to your offering, how can you
encourage your clients to consume your products
or services in new ways? If you have a personal
offering could it be repurposed to businesses? If

you have a business offering could you repurpose it to personal clients?

An example

Cereal is the example here. It's transitioned from a breakfast only food to a snack and something that can be enjoyed at any time of the day. By educating consumers and encouraging them to enjoy their favourite cereal at any time, the consumption and sales go up.

Try this:

You can begin by looking at the opposite of the marketplace where you sell and how your offering is consumed. Factors such as date, time, weather, gender and more can be flipped to find new potential buyers and repurposing success.

In this spirit, we have creating Clear Dating Message for singletons looking to portray themselves in the best light.

https://www.clearsalesmessage.com/clear-dating-message/

See also:

- How People Work > WYSIWYG
- How to Get Attention > The Show and Tell Effect

The Education Effect

- *It's the one thing you learnt today.*

What is it?

The Education Effect is when you are able to change your potential buyer's thinking by educating them in some way.

Why does it work?

It works because once we learn something new, or understand something we already know in a new way it creates intrigue, insight and has the ability to engage us in a new way. In the same way, the Von Restorff Effect describes that things in bold stand out, the same is true of unique or intriguing ideas and information.
New ideas and information stand out – especially those that positively challenge our thinking and educate us.

How can you use it?

Can you get "back to basics" when talking about "how" your offering works or how the needs of your buyers work? You may find that by covering areas you presume your buyers know, you will be providing new information and educating them in some way.

An example

HubSpot is the example here. HubSpot are an online tools provider for marketers. Many people first come across them because they find a post or a free pdf which includes educational content that is of value. Once the educational content has been read and its value proven, you are more likely to remember and engage with HubSpot.

Try this:

Can you include "how to" style content in your marketing, or perhaps explain "why" certain things occur for your buyers with their specific needs?

See also:

- How People Work > WYSIWYG
- How People Work > The Law of Past Experience
- How to Get Attention > The Show and Tell Effect
- How to Engage > The Scoring Effect

The Speed Effect

- *The quicker way to engage clients.*

What is it?

How quickly you deliver value to clients can be an important factor to engage them and help convert to sale.

Why does it work?

It works because as human beings we follow <u>the Path of Least Resistance</u> - we want to meet our needs and solve our problems in the quickest, simplest, easiest way possible. By focussing on just how quickly you can deliver value, solve a problem or do what you do, you can appeal to the innate need in all of us to just get things done.

How can you use it?

Depending on your offering, is there a part of what you do that can be delivered quickly? Something that would be appealing to clients as well as simple to complete in a given period of time? Focussing on part of your offering or the offering overall and how long it takes can be a paradigm shift in engaging clients who may otherwise falsely expect things to take much longer. It's a variant of <u>WYSIWYG</u> - if you don't tell them, they won't know.

An example

The best example here would be photo processing. Before digital cameras you needed to visit a shop to have them print the photos for you. Some outlets boasted 1hr photo processing, whereas others 4hrs or even 24hrs. Given the choice you'd pick the quickest one every time.

Try this:

Use how long it takes you to deliver value in your messaging. Is it one day, one week or 5 minutes? Being clear about the time it takes for your clients to get results is important and if that time is impressively short that's even better.

See also:

• How People Work > The Path of Least Resistance

The ECO Effect

- ***Good for the planet, great for the bottom line.***

What is it?

By focussing on the "Green" credentials that your offering or your company have, you can engage new buyers and differentiate from the "non-Green" competitors.

Why does it work?

It works because the concern with protecting our environment and ensuring everything we do is sustainable will only become more pervasive over time. Adapting your offering so that it's sustainably made, free from things that aren't good for the environment or in some way considerate of the planet will encourage faith in potential buyers.

How can you use it?

If you have a physical product, then adapting how it is made and transported so that it does have Green credentials is an essential move. In the short term, it helps sales, but in the long term the rules around material supply and transportation will only become stricter.

If you offer a service, then having a "carbon neutral" office or making donations to "Green" charities for each purchase will help to offset the potential negatives and ensure you appear "Green".

An example

In the UK, coffee shops will encourage you to use your own cup and discount the purchase to ensure you make the right choice for the environment. If you choose a cup, then you pay extra and that money goes to "Green" Initiatives.

Try this:

The simplest way to have "Greener" credentials is to support a "Green" charity with every sale you make. Find the most appropriate organisation, set up the donations and publicise your actions to your clients.

See also:

- How to Engage > The Identity Effect
- How to Engage > The "I have a Dream" Effect

The Nostalgia Effect

- *An engaging trip down memory lane.*

-

What is it?

The Nostalgia Effect is the act of recalling the past to engage your potential clients.

Why does it work?

It works because nostalgia comes to us all. We all like to remember "the good old days" and "the way things were", so when a business, product or service pays homage to a long-lost time it can immediately strike a chord with us and be something of interest and pleasure.

How can you use it?

Can you reference the past by using older branding or marketing collateral you may have once used? Create an image of a time that has past that will connect with your buyers and reflect positively on your brand. Perhaps look at how far things have come in terms of innovation and design to contrast your offering today with the primitive offering from long ago.

An example

Brands such as Coca Cola often use their older style of branding and bottles in their marketing. An iconic brand such as Coca Cola only needs to reference themselves rather than popular culture as they are so prevalent in daily life.

Try this:

Depending on your offering, think about how you can connect to past events in a positive way that will resonate with your clients. If your business is long established, then this can mean reverting back to older branding and offerings. If your business has no such history to refer to, then think about how your offering highlights fond memories of the past.

See also:

- How People Work > The Established Effect
- How People Work > The Law of Past Experience
- How to Engage > The Heritage Effect

The Heritage Effect

- *Your history can influence your future.*

What is it?

The Heritage Effect is about using the history and origins of your offering to your advantage.

Why does it work?

Businesses with a long history are perceived as more stable and reliable which can be a great selling point and differentiator (The Established Effect). The Heritage Effect looks not only at your history, but what that means for your buyers. Have you been developing and refining what you do for many years? did you invent something in your space or define your industry? Whilst you don't need to be the first or best, a compelling story surrounding the company or offering can help to engage potential buyers.

How can you use it?

Depending on your business and your offering, is there anything in your heritage and history that would be of interest to potential buyers? Did you create, refine or invent something new? Did you pioneer a new way of working in your industry? What have you achieved in the past that would have an impact on the buying decisions of your present clients?

An example

Mercedes-Benz invented the car in the 1800s. They use this innovation and the other innovations they have created to link the past to the present day and demonstrate the level of change and advancement they have pioneered in the automotive space.

Try this:

Talking about how long you have been in business, when you were established or the sheer number of clients you have served is a great way to take advantage of your company's heritage.

See also:

- How People Work > The Established Effect
- How to Engage > The Nostalgia Effect

The Business User Effect

- *Tailoring to business buyers wins business.*

What is it?

The Business User Effect is all about tailoring your offering to b2b clients and making it easier for them to buy.

Why does it work?

It works because some business buyers might actually need you to accommodate certain things such as payment terms or bulk / continuous orders. Whatever your offering, if you can't meet some basic requirements for business buyers then it's a case of they can't buy from you rather than they won't. By adapting to business buyers, you are harnessing The Path of Least Resistance and making it as easy as possible for them to choose you.

How can you use it?

If you have a large enough base of business buyers, adapt your offering to their needs and "specialise" for business clients with something that will appeal to them.

An example

Amazon have developed Amazon business to combine the benefits of shopping at Amazon with some of the necessary elements business buyers are looking for.

Try this:

If you have lots of B2B clients, then consider creating a slightly different option for them that appeals to what they need. VAT exclusive pricing, easy invoicing, payment accounts and bulk discounts are all appreciated by corporate clients.

See also:

- How to Engage > The Exclusive Effect
- How to Convert > The Qualify Effect
- How to Convert > The Buy More Effect

The Gift Effect

- *If you don't want it... maybe someone else will?*

What is it?

The Gift Effect is all about suggesting an offering as "the ideal gift" for someone else.

Why does it work?

It works for two reasons. Firstly, it gives the offering a second chance to be sold as even if the person seeing the communication doesn't want it, they may well buy it for a friend. Secondly, by suggesting something as a gift you are reframing the offering and making the potential buyer see it in a new way - this increases your chance of making the sale as you are making the buying decision simpler.

How can you use it?

Depending on your offering, could you take an item or service and reframe it as "the ideal gift"? Who would it be for? why might they want it? who might buy it for them? Some of your offering may sell much better as a gift instead of being bought by the actual consumer.

An example

Toiletries are often packaged as gift sets with the express purpose to be sold to someone who will gift the item. It doesn't make sense to buy a toiletry gift set for yourself, but as a gift they make something simple seem more luxurious.

Try this:

Is there any part of your offering that isn't selling so well? Take this product or service and see if you can re-package it as a gift for a loved one for XYZ occasion. By reframing as a gift, you reinvigorate the offer and maximise your chances of making the sale.

See also:

- How People Work > The Treat Effect
- Communication Basics > The Framing Effect
- How to Get Attention > The Christmas Effect
- How to Engage > The Should Effect

The Personification Effect

- *Using fictional characters to make real world sales.*

What is it?

The Personification Effect is where a fictional character is used or something inanimate is personified to create a recognisable character.

Why does it work?

It works because when something is personified, it alters how we interact with it. You will feel very differently about a Dyson vacuum cleaner than a Henry Hoover, because not only does the Henry Hoover have a name it has a face.

How can you use it?

There are two ways to put this to use. The first is to create a fictional character for your offering (think Ronald McDonald). The second way is to personify something inanimate (such as Henry Hoover). The question to answer would be - is it possible/appropriate to create name part of your offering and create a character? Would this enhance engagement for your potential clients or would it alienate them?

An example

From Henry Hoover to Ronald McDonald there are
countless examples of the Personification Effect at
work.
There is also a fascinating TED talk on the subject
of having emotional connections to inanimate
things.
Check out Kate Darling's TED talk on our
emotional connection to robots on YouTube.

Try this:

The simplest way to try this is to create a character
in your marketing (such as Ronald McDonald) who
personify everything you stand for. What would
they look like? What would they say? Would they
be a person, animal or a personified object? Have
fun and experiment within the boundaries of your
professional brand.

See also:

- How People Work > Emotion Trumps Logic
- How to Get Attention > The Bizarreness Effect
- How to Engage > The Empathy Effect

The Scoring Effect

- *Tangible scores provide a tangible point of engagement.*

What is it?

The Scoring Effect is about providing your clients with a tangible way to measure their need for your offering.

Why does it work?

It works because not only are we human beings competitive, we're also curious and seek outside measurement and approval to understand where we are in life, love and work. By providing a scoring mechanism to potential clients you not only tap into these competitive behaviours, but you display confidence, certainty and expertise as you are the expert grading the client and advising on improvement.

How can you use it?

Depending on your offering, can you provide your clients with a simple set of questions and a score out of 25/50/100 to measure their current position and advise on how it may be improved? LinkedIn use the SSI score as a means of grading your performance on LinkedIn and understanding what to do to improve.

How could you help your clients rate themselves and understand where they are now, whilst telling them how to improve and thus inspiring them with the confidence that you are the one to help them?

An example

The best example is the LinkedIn SSI Score. If you are a member of LinkedIn, check it out and see how LinkedIn rank your performance and provide suggestions for improvement.

Try this:

Create a simple set of questions that are the most critical things your clients need to have or do to get the result they seek. Allow your clients to rate themselves using this system and offer your advice on how to improve as a means of engagement.

See also:

- Communication Basics > The Inverted Pyramid Effect
- Communication Basics > The Facts and Figures Effect
- Communication Basics > Confidence. Certainty. Expertise.
- How to Get Attention > The Logic Effect
- How to Engage > FOMO
- How to Engage > The Education Effect
- How to Convert > The Qualify Effect

Lagniappe

- *Engagement doesn't stop just because they've bought...*

What is it?

Lagniappe is a fancy word used to describe the extra mile - it's an unexpected "gift" presented at the point of purchase.

Why does it work?

It works because when clients buy they expect to receive what they're paying for and no more. To receive something extra is a welcome surprise and helps to cement the buyer's decision to buy.

How can you use it?

Depending on your offering, what could you offer your clients by way of a small gift at the point of purchase that will be of low cost to you but high value or novelty to your buyer?

An example

Restaurants are the most common example here. Chocolates with the bill or a free desert/drink/snacks are common place.

Try this:

One of the simplest things you can offer as a
Lagniappe is an accessory or additional item or
service that the client will need once they've bought
from you. If you sell tools, then a free pair of safety
goggles or gloves would be a great Lagniappe and
for the minimal cost of the items themselves it
would make you stand out.

See also:

- Communication Basics > Positive Feedback Loop
- How to Engage > The Gift Effect
- How to Convert > The Free Gift Effect

The User Generated Content Effect

- *Allowing your clients to shape your business.*

What is it?

The User Generated Content Effect encourages your clients/users to add their creativity and perspective to your offering on social media.

Why does it work?

It works because it demonstrates that as a seller you care for your clients as you are seeking their input, but more importantly, it allows you to better understand how your offering is utilised in the "real world" and perhaps how it can even be improved or adapted.

How can you use it?

You can engage your clients on social media by asking them to share their experience of your brand or even to make suggestions or requests for future improvements.

An example

A relevant example of this would be the Starbucks White Cup Contest where social media users were encouraged to decorate the plain White Starbucks cup and share their creation online.

Try this:

There are two approaches you can take here. The first is to engage your clients by asking them to share their experience of your brand and perhaps even their own creativity as with the Starbucks example. The second is to get your clients to shape your business through their ideas and suggestions. Lego allows anyone to create and suggest model sets which are voted for online. This crowdsourced approach to product design ensures new Lego sets already have latent demand before they are launched.

See also:

- Hot to Get Attention > The Personalised Effect
- How People Work > Emotion Trumps Logic
- How to Engage > Loss Aversion

Trigger Point

- *If you want to hit your target, you need to find the trigger.*

What is it?

The Trigger Point is the circumstance that drives your client to need your offering.

Why does it work?

It works because most businesses understand their avatar; the ideal client they are seeking but very few understand when they need their ideal client. It makes sense that you speak to the right person at the right time to maximise your chance of making the sale. By identifying the trigger point you ensure that you are speaking with the client at the moment they need your offering.

How can you use it?

Look at your current and past clients and try to identify the circumstances they experienced just before making a purchase. Look for patterns and commonalities to create a blueprint of characteristics to help you identify future clients at precisely the right moment. Trigger points can be a definitive date in the calendar such as 31st January, an event such as a birth, death or

marriage, the can be a lack or abundance of something- or finally, a trigger can be an emotion.

An example

The simplest example of a trigger point would be a leaky tap. A leaky tap is the trigger point for needing a plumber, so using this in their messaging a plumber can make a more meaningful connection with potential clients.

Try this:

Identify your client's trigger point and then communicate with them at that time and location with a suitable message. Appeal to any emotional connection that might be attached to the trigger and the negative consequences of inaction.

See also:

- How People Work > Emotion Trumps Logic
- How to Engage > Loss Aversion

How to Convert

From engagement to sealing the deal.

Once you have the attention and engagement of your potential buyer, you then need to think about converting them to a sale.

The following "effects" look at how you can encourage a prospect to become a buyer, this is achieved largely by eliminating the unknowns and providing reassurance.

Your prospects are in fact looking for three things when they are in a sales conversation that will cause them to proceed to purchase or to abandon: Confidence, expertise and certainty.

These three elements need to exist together for a successful sale to be made; if any of them are missing the sale will almost certainly not proceed.

This is the shortest section of the book as much of the "heavy lifting" is completed when you are seeking to obtain the attention of a potential client and to then engage them.

Whilst what follows can be used to engage clients and seize their attention, these particular "effects" are focussed on making the sale and offer a commercially viable point of view.

It's time to make the sale.

Zero Risk Bias

- *Minimum risk = maximum chance of making the sale.*

What is it?

The Zero Risk Bias looks at the natural preference towards things which carry minimal to zero risk.

Why does it work?

By mitigating risk factors we can engage clients and encourage them to buy. Connecting to the potential fears of clients and tackling them head on will ensure they don't become obstacles to making the sale.

How can you use it?

Offering money back guarantees, providing free delivery and using client testimonials are three simple ways you can reassure your clients that your product or service is a low risk option for them.

An example

The example here would be the modern foam mattress companies who offer free delivery, money back guarantees and free collection. If you aren't happy, you are no worse for having bought the mattress and as such there is no risk.

Try this:

If possible, could you offer a full money back guarantee for your offering? Allow your clients a certain amount of time to make their mind up and then if they are not happy you refund them in full.

See also:

- How to Get Attention > The Star Effect
- How to Engage > Loss Aversion
- How to Engage > FOMO
- How to Engage > The Security Effect
- How to Convert > The Promise Effect
- How to Convert > The Freedom Effect
- How to Convert> The Pay on Results Effect
- How to Convert > Money Back Guarantee

Social Proof

- *If we see others buy and approve, we are more likely to buy.*

What is it?

Social Proof is the act of using reviews and comments from other clients to reassure and attract potential new clients.

Why does it work?

It works because if you are considering buying something, the reviews and comments of others can help to fill in the gaps as well as reassure you that you are not alone in "taking the risk" and buying the product or service.

How can you use it?

Using third party review sites such as Google, TripAdvisor, Trust Pilot and others is a credible way to request and collate the honest and unbiased comments of your clients.

Using case studies and testimonials can provide a more in depth and contextual example for potential new clients, reassuring them of how your product or service works, as well as the fact that others are also buying.

An example

Amazon is the example here. When buying anything on the site, but especially books, we can access a number of client reviews to help us make our mind up. Those items with more reviews and more positive reviews are more likely to sell as they are perceived to be the "safer" option.

Try this:

If you don't already, sign up to a review website or start collecting Google, Facebook or LinkedIn reviews from every client you deal with. The more reviews you have, the easier it will become to close clients as you have real world proof that your offering works.

See also:

- How People Work > Confirmation Bias
- How People Work > The Authority Effect
- Communication Basics > Confidence. Certainty. Expertise.
- How to Get Attention > The Like & Share Effect
- How to Get Attention > The Star Effect
- How to Get Attention > The Award-Winning Effect
- How to Engage> The Bandwagon Effect
- How to Engage> The Bystander Effect

- How to Engage> The Should Effect
- How to Engage> The Also Bought Because Effect
- How to Convert> The Bandwagon Effect

The Scarcity Effect

- ***Less is more.***

What is it?

The Scarcity Effect is when we are more inclined to take action and to do so without delay if there is a lack of time or resource available.

Why does it work?

It works because of FOMO - the Fear of Missing Out. If there are limited supplies or a limited timescale to act, then we have to make a decision and make it quickly. This decision will be focussed on not missing out where possible.

How can you use it?

If you want to drive engagement then put time limits on your offers or limit the supply of your products and services. This will create a pent-up demand and ensure those who want to act, will do so with haste as they do not want to miss out.

For example, "we have 3 spots remaining on our latest online training academy- click here to secure your spot!"

An example

Car sales often involves time specific deals which run out and limited supplies of vehicles. The limited availability of the discount is more likely to drive you to buy than if there was no limit at all.

Try this:

Could you run a time limited promotion for your offering that isn't based on supply, but based on time? Notice how the scarcity of time encourages more people to act than not.

See also:

- How to Get Attention > The Events Effect
- How to Engage > Loss Aversion
- How to Engage > FOMO
- How to Convert > The Qualify Effect
- How to Convert > The Happy Hour Effect

The Bare Minimum Effect

- *It's the least you can do.*

What is it?

Offering your clients the ability to purchase from you in the smallest and cheapest way possible to maximise the chance of them making a purchase.

Why does it work?

It works because your clients are naturally risk averse. By allowing someone the ability to work with you or sample your offering in the smallest way possible gives them a chance to test if you meet their standards and to experience your offering before they potentially buy more.

How can you use it?

Think about the smallest possible version of your offering you could have. Without damaging your main offering or brand, what's the cheapest, smallest offering you could present to the marketplace?

Add

An example

In the UK, many savings accounts are advertised as "invest from just £1" to signify that anyone can open an account and benefit from the savings rate on offer.

Try this:

If you don't already, make it clear the amount or scope of your offering in terms of minimums and maximums. What's the lowest order volume and what's the maximum order volume? (if there is one).

See also:

- How People Work > WYSIWYG
- How to Convert > The Mini Pack Effect
- How to Convert > The Loss Leader Effect

The Free Gift Effect

- *A giveaway can give your sales a boost.*

What is it?

Offering a "free gift" with a purchase can encourage a client to buy because they feel like they're getting a "better deal".
Why does it work?
It works because we all want value for money and to feel like we've had a lot more value than we've paid for. When we buy something, and get a "free gift", often that gift is no related or is essentially worthless to us, but the principle of getting "something for nothing" can drive us to buy.

How can you use it?

There are a couple of ways:

> **Free information products**
> Offering free information is a "zero cost" thing to do, has a high perceived value and is scalable. It also helps to create more trust and respect in the relationship you have with your clients.

Free physical products

In a physical product world, offering something for "free" that costs you money can seem counter intuitive.

But.

If you could increase your conversions by spending another £1/£5/£10 on a "free gift" it will have more impact than discounting by that amount.

As an added bonus, the "free gift" could be merchandise branded with your name, or products another company provide to you for free, to promote their business.

Free support

Offering ongoing "support" for a time period after purchase can encourage a buyer as they feel that you genuinely care about them and their purchase. If the client does call on you for support, it's your chance to shine and perhaps sell them something else. If they don't then you've lost nothing. Win. Win.

Free "upgrade"

If you have a higher priced offering, then rather than discount it, you can offer your clients a "free upgrade" to that offer for the price of the offering they were going to buy.

An example

For example, you sell umbrellas - one is a basic £5 model and one is a £10 deluxe model. In this scenario, you could offer a "free upgrade" to the deluxe model for all purchases before XYZ date.

This allows you to close the client, still make a margin (albeit a lesser one) and create word of mouth referral for your time limited deal. (see the Scarcity Effect)

Try this:

What could you give to clients that would be of little or no cost to you but would be valued by them? By adding value and providing more at the point of sale - even if the free thing isn't relevant to the purchase, you can convert more people.

See also:

- How to Get Attention > The Like & Share Effect
- How to Get Attention > Freemium
- How to Engage > The Law of Reciprocity
- How to Engage > Lagniappe
- How to Convert > The First Purchase Effect
- How to Convert > The Cashback Effect
- How to Convert > The No Brainer Effect
- How to Convert > The Loyalty Effect
- How to Convert > The Prize Draw Effect
- How to Convert > The Kids Go Free Effect

The Deal Effect

- *Everyone loves a deal.*

What is it?

Offering your clients "deals" and bundled offers can help to increase their engagement and likelihood of buying.

Why does it work

It works because often these "deals" offer better value to the client and are presented in a way that is simple to understand. If you do the "thinking" for your client and make it as easy as possible to buy from you, then you are more likely to make the sale.

Deals can also lead clients to buy more with the money "they have saved" by buying your better value bundled offering - they can be a form of entry into buying your other offerings.

How can you use it

If you have a number of different products or services, could you bundle some of them together into logical groups that appeal to your clients? Perhaps a "starter kit" or "specialist bundle" or "ultimate collection". By curating your offering and displaying it in the simplest terms possible you will make it easier for your clients to buy.

An example

McDonalds Happy Meal and value meals are an everyday example of this in action. Not only is the cost of the meal less than the sum of the individual elements, it encourages you to buy a drink and fries - not just a burger. They have defined what a "meal" consists of in terms of fast food.

Try this:

Create an offer which combines elements of your offering together into a package. Make that package price less than the sum of the parts (but still profitable for you). Promote the package as a whole and you should find that buyers opt for the deal rather than the individual elements which means they spend more with you overall.

See also:

- How People Work > The Path of Least Resistance
- How to Convert > The Buy More Effect
- How to Convert > The Points Effect
- How to Convert > The Finance Effect
- How to Convert > The Trade in Effect
- How to Convert > The Subscription Effect
- How to Convert > The Discount Effect
- How to Convert > The Mega Pack Effect
- How to Convert > The Early Bird Effect
- How to Convert > The No Brainer Effect

- How to Convert > The Kids Go Free Effect

See also: Psychology of Price

The numbers you use in your deals can have an impact on your buyer and drive their engagement and decision making.

The Finance Effect

- *Expensive is relative.*

What is it?

The Finance Effect looks at the simple matter of making your offering financially affordable to your potential clients by providing different ways to pay.

Why does it work?

It works because as buyers we can often want something but simply don't have the money. By offering finance or flexible payment options you can ensure that those who want to buy are able to do so and not deterred through lack of funds. Of all the objections and reasons to lose the sale, lack of funds is both a common and easily handled situation, but if you aren't prepared for it, or if you don't make it clear then the client may never ask.

How can you use it?

Remembering that expensive is relative, look at your offering. It's not just the items that cost thousands that are out of reach to some of your potential clients.

For anything that is greater in price than £100 or $100 can you offer a flexible payment plan or partner with a third-party finance provider?

An example

In the UK, the sofa industry is nearly entirely driven by finance and monthly payments. In the advertising and messaging used, we are told how we can have amazing new furniture from just 50p per week for XX weeks rather than for £2000 which would be the retail price.

Try this:

If you have issues with clients affording your offering, then team up with a company to help create a payment plan. PayPal and other online card providers offer the service, or you could go for something more tailor made.

See also:

- How People Work > The Path of Least Resistance
- How to Convert > The Subscription Effect
- How to Convert > The Deal Effect
- How to Convert > The Buy Now Pay Later Effect

See also: Psychology of Price

The numbers you use in your finance monthly payments can have an impact on your buyer and drive their engagement and decision making.

The Qualify Effect

- *We only sell to certain people...*

What is it?

The Qualify Effect occurs when we can't simply buy something. In order to buy we need to meet some criteria and are essentially left "asking" the seller to sell to us.

Why does it work?

It works because of <u>Reactance</u>. When we are told we can't do something, it spurs us on to do it. But more than that, the Qualify Effect helps to separate the serious buyers from the "tyre kickers". It ensures that those who are serious have to make a commitment (by jumping through hoops) before they are given the opportunity to buy.

How can you use it?

Using the Qualify Effect in your sales process is simple enough to implement. Decide on your "ideal" client type and then make this clear in your sales conversations. "We typically deal with businesses of at least 5 people and a £2M turnover

- can I just check your company meets that please?"

Asking in this way puts you in the upper hand and ensures that if the client doesn't meet the criteria, they can't proceed.

An example

Credit cards have different levels of offering for different clients. You need to be of a certain criterion to get an Amex Platinum or Centurion card. As such they are desirable and coveted by those who don't have them.

Try this:

Define your ideal client type and focus on a criterion that will make a difference in what they buy from you. Is it their need? Their budget? Or the size of their business? Create a minimum standard for them to hit and then use it. For example, we only sell sales books to people who have at least £14.99 and an internet connection ☺

See also:

- How to Engage > The Exclusive Effect
- How to Engage > FOMO
- How to Engage > The Business User Effect
- How to Engage > The Scoring Effect
- How to Convert > The Scarcity Effect

The No Brainer Effect

- *Make it a no brainer decision.*

What is it?

The No Brainer Effect looks at engaging prospects by offering something that is "too good to be true". The value of what you are offering seems to massively outweigh the asking price and/or the proposition could be a win/win for all parties involved. With the No Brainer Effect, your buyer will struggle to see any reason not to make the purchase and feel compelled to buy.

Why does it work?

It works because as buyers not only do we want to secure as much "stuff" as possible (even if we don't need it), but we also want to feel like we got a great deal and a great ROI (return on investment) for what we are spending. Where the value of the offering appears to massively outweigh the price it also justifies our purchasing decision and eliminates our responsibility should anything go wrong. After all who wouldn't want to buy £150 worth of Makeup for just £29?

How can you use it?

Using the No Brainer Effect in your business involves either creating a deal or offer where you bundle together products or services with a high combined value and offer it for a much lesser price or you find a way to present your offering that benefits all parties or has multiples benefits to it – a Win/Win Scenario.

An example

A great example of this would be magazine subscriptions. You get xx copies of the magazine for much less than the price of buying it in a shop and you also get some kind of special gift such as toiletries or accessories. The total value of what you are getting far outweighs the price - why wouldn't you subscribe? it's a No Brainer!
The No Brainer Effect combines the Deal Effect, The Free Gift Effect and The Abundance Effect to created something irresistible After all- you wouldn't want to miss out.... would you?

Try this:

Create an offer which combines elements of your offering together into a package. Make that package price less than the sum of the parts (but still profitable for you). Promote the package as a whole and you should find that buyers opt for the deal rather than the individual elements which means they spend more with you overall.

See also:

- How People Work > The Path of Least Resistance
- How People Work > The Abundance Effect
- How to Convert > The Deal Effect
- How to Convert > The Free Gift Effect
- How to Convert > The Pay on Results Effect
- How to Convert > Money Back Guarantee

The Loyalty Effect

- *Loyalty is rewarding.*

What is it?

Using loyalty points and rewards to incentivise buyer behaviour.

Why does it work?

It works because as humans we repeat rewarded behaviour. When our loyalty to a particular brand is rewarded we respond by repeating that behaviour.

How can you use it?

By simply creating a loyalty card or offering loyalty points and discounts you can ensure clients think twice about buying anywhere else. It's rewarding their behaviour to buy from you that is the primary goal.

An example

Air miles is the most world-renowned example of a loyalty system. By rewarding passengers with air miles to redeem against flights the airlines can sell more tickets (as air miles + cash is the most common transaction) as well as making those people feel like they are getting a great deal and their loyalty is being rewarded.

Try this:

Depending on your offering, create a simple loyalty system that rewards the client with something free as a thank you. It could be as simple as a card stamping system in a coffee shop.

See also:

- How to Convert > The Points Effect
- How to Convert > The Free Gift Effect
- How to Convert > The Subscription Effect
- How to Convert > The Promise Effect
- How to Convert > The With-Purchase Effect

The Prize Draw Effect

- *Winning new clients through competitions.*

What is it?

The Prize Draw Effect occurs when offering the chance to win something encourages more people to buy.

Why does it work?

It works because we love to get "more than we bargained for" which is a mixture of The Abundance Effect and The Free Gift Effect. Potential buyers who are undecided can be moved towards conversion with the promise of (potentially) extra value and deliverables. If you were looking to buy something and nearly decided, a prize draw can help to seal the deal and also make the purchase a "no brainer" – not only do you get the product/service - you might also win a trip to see Willy Wonka!

How can you use it?

If appropriate to your offering, you can offer a prize to those purchasing your product/service within a given timeframe. The prize doesn't need to be relevant to your offering; the more attractive and universally appealing the prize, the more likely a prospect will buy.

An example

In consumer goods, we are often bombarded with "instant win" promotions and special prizes. There are too many great examples to name but Willy Wonka has to be the most well-known and successful use of the effect.

Try this:

Choosing an arbitrary prize such as an iPad, run a competition for the next xxx days encouraging people to "like and share" a piece of your content on social media. Not only will you get the increased reach and visibility from the sharing, you will have only paid the cost of the iPad for the privilege.

See also:

- How to Get Attention > Freemium
- How to Engage > Lead Magnet
- How to Convert > The Free Gift Effect
- How to Convert > The First Purchase Effect
- How to Convert > The Early Bird Effect

The Freedom Effect

- ***Stay because you want to, not because you have to.***

What is it?

The Freedom Effect is about allowing your clients complete freedom in how and when they buy from you without penalty. Some mobile phone operators and online companies offer an "upgrade or downgrade at any time" approach to their pricing model – with no penalties. This places the focus on their confidence in the quality of the offering. If they let their offering speak for itself rather than use penalties to keep you on board, it must be good.

Why does it work?

It works because not only do we want to minimise risk as buyers, we also don't want to be trapped into long term contracts or feel like we're not in control.

How can you use it?

Can you make your pricing model one that can be upgraded or downgraded at any time without penalty? Can you allow clients to cancel at any time and just pay for what they have used rather than incur a penalty or make them wait 30 days?

This is more suited to businesses with ongoing or recurring billing – in the case of one time purchases, you can consider offering some kind of guarantee for peace of mind that will create the same sense of freedom.

An example

Netflix allows you to leave at any time. Unlike other TV subscriptions there are no contracts or tie ins - you stay subscribed to Netflix because it's a great service and you want to, not because you are tied in.

Try this:

If you have a subscription based model, then offer your clients the ability to cancel at any time. This bold move will not only communicate confidence about your offering, but will attract new clients who were previously wary of being tied in to longer term contracts.

See also:

- How to Engage > The Empathy Effect
- How to Convert > Zero Risk Bias

The Trade in Effect

- *It's time for an upgrade.*

What is it?

The Trade in Effect is when you offer a discount to a client when they bring their old product to you when they purchase.

Why does it work?

It works because we naturally want to have the latest, bestest, most shiniest things possible and by offering a trade in this is not only made possible, but made cheaper.

How can you use it?

This is best suited to a physical product offering, so what discount could you offer clients in return for them bringing their old/used/faulty items to you when they purchase.

An example

The car industry use this approach widely as it's very relevant to their marketplace. Selling a car, getting the money and then using that to buy a new car can be a disjointed process. It's much more convenient to sell your car to the dealer as a

"trade in" against a newer model. You know the deal might not be the best but it's convenient and in that instance, that's what appeals the most.

Try this:

This works for physical products rather than services, so think about the trigger point that drives your clients to buy - is it a broken product? Old product? Something that is no longer fit for purpose? Find your "angle" such as broken products and then target those people by offering a direct trade in on the faulty product which results in a discount against its replacement.

See also:

- How People Work > Shiny Object Syndrome
- How to Get Attention > The New Version Effect
- How to Convert > The Deal Effect

The Subscription Effect

- *We're in it for the long haul.*

What is it?

The Subscription Effect is when you offer your clients a discount in return for them committing to buy from you repeatedly / over the long term.

Why does it work?

It works because not only can you offer your clients a better deal in return for their commitment, but you have the assurance of their ongoing loyalty and custom. Clients appreciate being able to "set it and forget it" and sit back safe in the knowledge that you will look after their needs on an ongoing basis.

How can you use it?

Depending on your offering, is it possible to create a subscription model or a recurring membership fee to give clients ongoing access to your offering and ensure you retain them over the longer term? For physical products with a limited lifespan you can offer a subscription for regular delivery of the product which is better value over time for the client so they get a deal.

For service based products, you can create groups and give access to resources for a period of time and charge for access.

An example

Amazon use this model for their consumable items. Many items are priced at 5-15% cheaper if you "subscribe and save" meaning you will buy more of the product on a more regular basis than simply a one off. Amazon get your loyalty and you get a better deal- win/win.

Try this:

If you have an advice/coaching/consulting based business, then consider creating a community or access to support and help as and when it's required. For a low monthly fee your clients can access the help they need and connect with likeminded people as well as engaging you for your full services as and when they are required.

See also:

- How to Convert > The Deal Effect
- How to Convert > The Loyalty Effect

The Refer a Friend Effect

- *Sharing your purchase can be rewarding.*

What is it?

The Refer a Friend Effect is when you offer an incentive to your existing clients to recommend your offering.

Why does it work?

It works because there are few things more powerful than a personal recommendation. There are also few things more motivating that being paid money to do something - especially something as simple as talking to your friends about a product or service you already enjoy.

How can you use it?

Think about your current client base. Would they be in touch with potential clients for your offering? If so can you offer them a financial or prize draw incentive to refer new potential clients to you?

An example

Uber is one of the most recent examples of this working very well indeed. Many of Uber's first riders were invited by friends. Those friends got a credit of £X for inviting the person and often the person who was invited also got something. Incentivising both parties in this way has helped Uber spread very quickly indeed – why wouldn't you recommend a service that works very well and pays you to recommend it?

Try this:

If appropriate, think about how you can financially incentivise your current client base to recommend you to their network. It could be money or gift cards - or better yet and cheaper for you to offer – a discount or something additional for free as part of your offering.

See also:

- How People Work > The Authority Effect

The Points Effect

- *What do points make? Conversions.*

What is it?

You can encourage buyers and maintain loyalty by offering points for each purchase. These points can then be exchanged for goods, cash or something else at a later date.

Why does it work?

It works because we are biased towards rewarded behaviour. It's a form of gamification- even if the cash value of the points is 20p, using 1000 points to incentivise behaviour will be more effective than simply offering a 20p discount.

How can you use it?

Depending on your offering, think about how you could incentivise buyers to take certain actions such as buying, subscribing or making a repeat purchase by rewarding their behaviour with points that can then be redeemed for cash, discounts or other goods. What would be the lowest cost to you, but of the highest value to your client?

An example

A great example of the Points Effect would be Tesco Clubcard in the UK where points can be used to buy vouchers for meals or days out.

Try this:

Create a points system for your offering and then establish tiers. Each tier provides the buyer with a perk such as a discount, free offer or other beneficial item as a reward for them amassing points.

See also:

- Communication Basics > Positive Feedback Loop
- How to Convert > The Loyalty Effect
- How to Convert > The Deal Effect

The Buy More Effect

- *The more you buy, the more you are rewarded.*

What is it?

You can encourage buyers to buy more by rewarding them for the more that they spend.

Why does it work?

It works for a number of reasons. Firstly, because we love to get a good deal when we buy things and if we buy more we get more which is attractive. Secondly it's a variation of the "In for a Penny" Effect where once we have decided to buy it's easier to decide to buy more - especially as it's being rewarded.

How can you use it?

Depending on your offering, think about how you could incentivise buyers to buy more – would it be to give them money off, extra points or extra "stuff". Create a reward for buying more, set the parameters of how much "more" is and experiment.

An example

In the UK, there are often many "Free £5 gift card when you spend £50 and Free £10 gift card when you spend £100" promotions. The more you spend with these retailers, the higher the value of gift card they provide you. It's a form of discounting but created to encourage a higher transaction value.

Try this:

If your offering involves multiple potential purchases, then you can offer your clients the chance to buy 1 for £x or 3 for £x. Creating a higher volume offering which represents greater value to the client is the goal here.

See also:

- How People Work > The Abundance Effect
- Communication Basics > Positive Feedback Loop
- How to Engage > The Premium Effect
- How to Convert > The Business User Effect
- How to Convert > The Deal Effect
- How to Convert > The With-Purchase Effect

The First Purchase Effect

- *Once they've had a taste...*

What is it?

The First Purchase Effect looks at discounting the first purchase to help new potential clients to buy from you.

Why does it work?

It works because many potential buyers are sceptical about making a purchase and "risking" their time and money on your offering. By lowering the price of the first purchase you are making it "less risky" for clients to buy but without discounting their expectation of the value of your offering overall.

How can you use it?

Depending on your offering, by discounting the first session, first purchase or first XX amount of time using your offering you can create a simpler and "less risky" way for clients to sample your offering before transitioning to full price.

An example

Netflix and other subscription services will offer you the first month for 99p or similar. By dramatically discounting the first purchase, they gain you as a client and once you experience the offering you should then decide to pay full price.

Try this:

If you have a consumable offering or subscription based offering, could you discount the first purchase to allow new clients to experience your offering with minimal risk?

See also:

- How People Work > Shiny Object Syndrome
- How to Get Attention > Freemium
- How to Engage > The Law of Reciprocity
- How to Convert > The Prize Draw Effect
- How to Convert > The Cashback Effect
- How to Convert > The Free Gift Effect
- How to Convert> The Buy Now Pay Later Effect
- How to Convert > The Loss Leader Effect

The Cashback Effect

- *It's discounting, but by another name.*

What is it?

An alternative to discounting, offering cash back has the same effect but without associating the offering with a "lower" price.

Why does it work?

It works because it encourages the buyer to buy in the same way a discount would; they get a great deal on an offering they need, but it doesn't affect how the price of the offering is perceived which makes everyone feel better. Discounting can make an offering feel "cheaper" and effect perception of value, but offering cash back avoids this entirely whilst achieving the same overall objective.

How can you use it?

Depending on your offering, think about how you could offer cash back and how much the cash back might be. This works best for physical products, but can apply to anything that you sell.
Will you offer £50, £100 or £500 cash back? over what time period? How should your buyer claim

it? Being clear on the details and if there are any qualifying criteria is essential to success.

An example

Mobile phone deals in the UK often come with a cashback element. Once you have committed to the contract, you are "refunded" a few weeks or months later. This ensures you stay as a client and you get rewarded for your purchase and loyalty.

Try this:

Instead of discounting, consider offering clients cashback or vouchers when they buy.

See also:

- How to Convert > The Free Gift Effect
- How to Convert > The First Purchase Effect
- How to Convert> The Buy Now Pay Later Effect

See also: Psychology of Price

The numbers you use for the cashback can have an impact on your buyer and drive their engagement and decision making.

The Discount Effect

- *The simplest but most dangerous way to sell more.*

What is it?

Discounting a purchase is one of the simplest and easiest ways to convert buyers.

Why does it work?

It works because it simply makes the offering cheaper. Whether as a sale item or through the use of a voucher code or other mechanism, making your offering cheaper makes it more appealing and accessible. But proceed with caution; offerings that are regularly discounted can be perceived differently as those which are offered at a lower price - tying the discount to a particular reason can discourage buyers from expecting a regular discount.

How can you use it?

Any offering can be discounted at any point but it's a potentially dangerous thing to do unless you use it sparingly. If you do choose to discount then be sure to associate the discount with an event, special deal or another outside factor that ensures your buyers don't expect a discount or perceive your offering differently.

An example

Black Friday is the most obvious example of arbitrary discounting. An American convention, Black Friday has become a universal opportunity to discount without the act of discounting effecting your offering.

Try this:

Use the anniversary of your business or your offering as a way to introduce a "birthday discount" to your offering. This allows you to reach and convert potentially more clients but without damaging how they perceive the cost of your offering.

How to frame the price:
There are a number of ways to reframe the price including:

Was £ then £ now £
Contrasting to previous sale / non-sale prices.

Save £
Highlighting the definitive saving in £ of a reduction

Save %
Highlighting the saving in % of a reduction

Only £ per x
Reframe the price per use
Starting from £
Identify the lowest entry price point.

Reduced to £
Identify the new low price point rather than the saving.

See also:

- How to Convert > The Cashback Effect
- How to Convert > The Deal Effect
- How to Convert > The Early Bird Effect

See also: Psychology of Price

The numbers you use in your discounts can have an impact on your buyer and drive their engagement and decision making.

The Mega Pack Effect

- ***Give your clients more of what they want at a great price.***

What is it?

Offering clients a bulk buy version of what you already offer, but at a discounted rate as they are purchasing more in one transaction.

Why does it work?

It works because buyers feel like they are getting a **deal** and that it's a **no brainer** to buy more of something they are going to be using anyway. As sellers, it allows us to sell more and have a larger transaction size as the client buys more than they intended.

How can you use it?

Depending on your offering, can you create a "Mega Pack" or "bulk" offering which includes more of what you already offer but at a discounted rate? An example

The simplest example here is washing powder. From time to time you will see "Mega Pack" boxes which contain a considerable amount more washing powder but at only a slightly higher price than the original offering.

Try this:

If you have a physical offering, then create a week/month/year supply of that offering at a competitive price and sell that to existing clients. If you have a service based offering, then allowing clients more access to support or allowing them to bulk buy their usage will have the same effect.

See also:

- How People Work > The Abundance Effect
- How to Engage > The Premium Effect
- How to Convert > The Deal Effect
- How to Convert > The Mini Pack Effect

The Mini Pack Effect

- *Create a smaller "bitesize" version of your offering.*

What is it?

The Mini Pack Effect is about creating a smaller, cheaper, "bitesize" version of your offering to entice potential clients to try.

Why does it work?

It works because as buyers we want the least amount of risk and the least amount of resistance. If a buyer is unsure about your offering and they are presented with an opportunity to purchase a smaller version at a much lower cost, then it's a more attractive proposition which could lead the buyer to then buy the "full" version too.

How can you use it?

Depending on your offering, consider how you can create a smaller, cheaper version. What could you remove or shrink down that wouldn't affect the quality of your offering, just the quantity?

An example

The simplest example here would be the "fun size" chocolates or "variety" packets of Kellogg's cereal. It allows you to enjoy the product in its smallest possible form.

Try this:

If you have a physical offering, then can you create a physically smaller or less feature laden version that you can offer at a lower price?
If you have an intangible/service driven offering what's the smallest thing you could do for a client that would benefit them but not expensive or time consuming so it can be offered at a bitesize price?

See also:

- How People Work > The Path of Least Resistance
- How People Work > The Framing Effect
- How to Convert > The Mega Pack Effect
- How to Convert > The Bare Minimum Effect

The Also Bought Effect

- ***People who bought this book also bought our Email Kit course ;-)***

What is it?

By telling your clients what other clients bought, you can encourage them to buy the same things.

Why does it work?

It works because we are likely to follow the behaviour and decisions of others - especially those in the same situation as us. It's likely that the things others bought are not only of interest to us, but necessary. It's also possible that we didn't even consider what else we may need so the suggestions may be welcomed and appreciated.

How can you use it?

Whether you have an online or offline offering a product or a service - you can advise your clients of the other things that previous buyers opted for. This not only maximises the value of the sale but can demonstrate confidence, certainty and expertise which are vital for closing any sale.

An example

Amazon is a great example of this in action. When you buy something on Amazon, they show you examples of what others bought- even if it's seemingly random.

Try this:

This is about curating your offering for your buyer. Think logically and carefully about what they might need next after they buy and the context behind why they are buying in the first place. Then offer it to them.

See also:

- Communication Basics > Confidence. Certainty. Expertise.
- How to Convert > Social Proof
- How to Convert > The With-Purchase Effect

The Comparison Effect

- *Comparison is the thief of joy, but the saviour when selling.*

What is it?

Providing clients with a comparison of your offering versus other versions of the offering and the competition can help clients make a better decision.

Why does it work?

It works because when we make it as easy as possible for our clients to understand and decide upon our offering, they are more likely to make a choice. By focussing on the most important elements of the offering we demonstrate that we understand what our buyers seek and give them the vital information they need to make a buying decision.

How can you use it?

There will be certain aspects of your offering that are the most important to your clients. If you don't know what these elements are then your clients can surely tell you. With a shortlist of the most important elements and an understanding of what your clients seek you can compare your offering to the competition and to other alternatives.

An example

The best example for this is Amazon. Many of the items they feature for sale are compared against the others to help you make the best buying decision possible.

Try this:

The next time you present your offering in person or online, select the factors that are most important to your client and compare those to your cheaper and more expensive versions and/or the competition. Allow your client to make the best decision for themselves by giving them the information they need.

See also:

- How People Work > The Path of Least Resistance
- Communication Basics > The Framing Effect
- How to Get Attention > The Price Per Use Effect
- How to Engage > Anchoring
- How to Engage > Equivalence

The Early Bird Effect

- *The early bird gets the deal.*

What is it?

The Early Bird Effect is a way of encouraging early adopters to purchase by offering a discount to reward their speed.

Why does it work?

It works because discounting is an effective way to get buyers to take action. Early bird discounts usually have a time limit, (Scarcity Effect) meaning that you need to act quickly which adds to the effectiveness of the method. Early Bird pricing can only ever be used when you first offer something for sale, it's ineffective and confusing to offer early bird deals on existing offerings.

How can you use it?

The next time you launch a new product, deal or service; consider offering early adopters a discount if they act within a certain time frame. You will get the clients; they will get a great deal and the overall perception of the value of your offering will not be affected.

An example

Travelling by train is a good example here. Often the best rates are those booked in advance. Early bird saver deals help train companies to secure the deal and provide passengers who plan ahead a great deal.

Try this:

Reach out to existing buyers or subscribers and offer them a discount on the next "new" thing you do. They will appreciate the exclusiveness of the offer and you will be more likely to close them.

See also:

- How to Get Attention > The Events Effect
- How to Convert > The Deal Effect
- How to Convert > The Discount Effect
- How to Convert > The Prize Draw Effect
- How to Convert > The Happy Hour Effect

The Price Match Effect

- *Same deal. Different seller.*

What is it?

The Price Match Effect is the act of literally matching your competitor's price to seal the deal.

Why does it work?

It works because often price is the only differentiating factor for buyers - especially in crowded or commoditised marketplaces. Differentiating on price is ill-advised as it not only eats into profit margins, it also attracts buyers who are only price loyal. That said, sometimes if you want to secure a deal or show some "goodwill" to secure a client with a potentially higher lifetime value, then matching the price is something in your arsenal. It's not just for high street retailers and online shops.

How can you use it?

You can use this in two ways. The first is to publicise in your messaging the fact that you will "match or beat any quote" or that you "won't be beaten on price". This will raise awareness to potential buyers but may damage your ability to maintain margins and focus on value over price - you are commoditising your offering but it will drive sales.

The second is to use it as a closing tool. When you are negotiation with a client you can offer to match a price "unexpectedly" to ensure you don't lose the business purely on cost. This can be more beneficial as you appear to be extending goodwill and favour to the client rather than trying to be the "cheapest" in the marketplace.

An example

Best Buy in the USA and numerous companies across the world have a "price match guarantee" which means they will match any genuine competitor price that meets certain criteria.

Try this:

The next time you find yourself in an overly competitive marketplace - try publicising the fact that you won't be beaten on price or will match a genuine competitor and notice the difference.

See also:

- How to Engage > Equivalence

The Checklist Effect

- *Ticking down to making the sale.*

✓ What is it?

The Checklist Effect is about highlighting,
summarising and repeating the most important
and compelling parts of your offer so that just
before purchasing your buyer has everything they
need to proceed.

✓ Why does it work?

It works because as buyers we naturally want
reassurance we are doing the right thing as we are
driven by a fear of loss and want to minimise risk.
By summarising and repeating the most important
parts at the very moment just before purchase we
have everything we need to make the best decision
possible. We are also likely to have forgotten some
of the "things" we get once we make the purchase
so this timely reminder is another nudge.

✓ How can you use it?

Just before a client buys, online or offline, have a checklist of the benefits and "stuff" they will get when they buy. This will help them to make their decision and ensure you have provided as much information and evidence as possible to make the case for why they should buy your offering.

✓ An example

Websites are awash with checklists - especially when it comes to pricing. As each price tier is laid out, the component parts of that price are split out so you know exactly what you are getting in terms of benefits and actual "stuff"

✓ Try this:

Make a checklist of the most important parts of your offering so that just before you make the sale online or offline you can summarise the most important and valuable reasons the buyer should buy.

✓ See also:

- How People Work > The Abundance Effect
- How People Work > WYSIWYG

The Promise Effect

- ***Our promise to you is that this helps conversion.***

What is it?

The Promise Effect is all about making (and keeping) promises to your clients about the things that matter to them.

Why does it work?

It works because for most buyers there are one or two compelling things that they really need or want. It's their fear of not getting those things or not being sure of an unknown that can lead them to not buy from you. By promising to deliver XYZ you bridge the gap between the unknowns a buyer is trying to solve and their decision to purchase.

How can you use it?

Find the most compelling thing you can promise to your buyer and make that promise. What is it that your buyers fear or aren't too sure about? If you can make a promise regarding this area in particular then you will engage and convert more clients as you demonstrate empathy and a commitment to them - you are on their team.

An example

Many food outlets and producers make promises about the ingredients they source; both where they are from and how they are sourced.

Try this:

What promise can you make to your clients that they will not only appreciate, but that may be enough to cause them to buy? Is it a promise about service levels, how quickly you operate or things you will or won't do that will align with their values?

See also:

- How to Convert > Zero Risk Bias
- How to Convert > The Loyalty Effect
- How to Convert > Money Back Guarantee

The Happy Hour Effect

- *Everyone's happy when they're paying less.*

What is it?

The Happy Hour Effect is all about encouraging clients to buy using time restricted pricing.

Why does it work?

It works because as buyers we are seeking the best deal and maximum value for money. If something we are considering buying will be more expensive later in the day simply because it's later in the day, then we are more compelled to buy now and secure a better deal.

How can you use it?

Depending on your offering, consider the slowest times of day or week in your business. Create a "Happy Hour" offer that provides a discount or something extra to incentivise clients to buy during those quiet times. The Happy Hour Effect works best for in-person, physical businesses such as bars and restaurants, but can be effective in any business if the offer is compelling enough.

An example

Many food outlets and bars have special reduced priced offerings for the downtimes. Few people eat their evening meal before 5pm but many restaurants will have cheaper options in these downtimes to attract customers.

Try this:

Create a 10% discount offer for a 2-hour window when you are at the most unlikely to sell to a client. This could be every Friday 5-7 or every day 10am-midday. To maximise effectiveness, you need to pick the most unlikely time for your clients to buy.

See also:

- Communication Basics > The Timely Effect
- How to Convert > The Scarcity Effect
- How to Convert > The Early Bird Effect

The Kids Go Free Effect

- ***Being a parent is expensive enough...***

What is it?

The Kids Go Free Effect is all about appealing to parents by making your offering free to their children.

Why does it work?

It works because as parents, life can be EXPENSIVE. If you are able to take your children somewhere for free it not only appeals to you as a parent as you feel like someone understands your financial pressures, but it means you actually spend less. For the outlet offering kids to go free, the reality is that children eat, drink and consume very little so the real cost of the offer is minimised.

How can you use it?

Depending on your offering, consider offering one child free per paying adult. Being clear on the paying adult is important as you need to charge someone money for your offering - it can't simply be free to all.

An example

Many food outlets and family attractions have "Kids Go Free" offers to attract parents.

Try this:

Depending on your offering, consider allowing kids to go for "free" when accompanied by a paying adult. Whatever the kids consume of your offering should be covered in the adult's payment and as such it should not be a loss-making exercise.

See also:

- How People Work > Path of Least Resistance
- How to Convert > The Deal Effect
- How to Convert > The Free Gift Effect

See also: Psychology of Colour

The colours you use can have an impact on your buyer and drive their engagement and decision making. The most commonly used colours to use for "Kid" things are often bold colours such as Red, Green, Blue and Yellow

The With-Purchase Effect

- *Existing buyers are more likely to buy again.*

What is it?

The With-Purchase Effect is all about further promotion once a buyer has purchased. It's the additional promotional material and offers made once somebody has bought.

Why does it work?

It works because people that buy are more likely to buy again or buy more. If you have just bought a toy you might want batteries, if you've bought a magazine on health then a leaflet about supplements makes sense. Offering logical upsells after a purchase has been made can encourage further revenue.

How can you use it?

If you ship physical products, include leaflets, vouchers and offers with the purchase.

If you sell intangible products/services, include offers and codes on email when you have confirmed the client's order has been placed.

An example

When you buy a package from Amazon you often get a Netflix offer or leaflets for a Wine Club or similar. Amazon are trying to make you feel special by offering you exclusive deals.

Try this:

Think about the logical additional purchases that may be required with your offering. Can you offer these items to your buyers when they buy to capture their attention and the sale at the right moment?

See also:

- How People Work> The Path of Least Resistance
- How to Engage > The Exclusive Effect
- How to Convert > The Loyalty Effect
- How to Convert > The Buy More Effect
- How to Convert > The Also Bought Effect

The Buy Now Pay Later Effect

- *Easing client cash flow concerns.*

What is it?

The Buy Now Pay Later Effect allows your buyers to make the purchase whilst delaying the payment date.

Why does it work?

It works because cash flow and affordability are an issue for many buyers- it allows clients to buy even if they can't "afford" it here and now. The ability to defer payments and or combine them with a finance plan can remove the barriers to making the purchase and secure a sale which may not otherwise have occurred.

How can you use it?

Depending on your offering, could you offer your clients the ability defer payment to after delivery to ease their cash flow? It's common for paying later to be combined with a finance offer so the client has a period of no repayments and then their finance repayments commence.

An example

The most common example would be the furniture industry. Sofas are often offered with "no payments for 12 months" or similar to encourage browsing clients to move to sale without having to raise the money they need.

Try this:

If you offer finance as part of your offering, could you include a deferred payment option for 3/6/12 months to allow any potential client to proceed today without money being a barrier?

See also:

- How to Convert> The Finance Effect
- How to Convert> The First Purchase Effect
- How to Convert> The Cashback Effect
- How to Convert> The Pay on Results Effect

The Pay on Results Effect

- *Only pay for what you get.*

What is it?

The Pay on Results Effect is about only charging clients for the deliverable result, not the amount of time and effort necessary to achieve the result.

Why does it work?

It works because as buyers we are seeking to minimise our risk. By only paying when you receive the result you desire, it not only means you can't lose, you also don't need to risk any of your money to achieve the result. It creates a no-brainer.

How can you use it?

This works for service based / intangible offerings rather than products. Depending on your offering, could you operate a "no win no fee" approach which incentivises your buyer to buy and you to succeed? So long as the downside and cost of not achieving the result for your client are outweighed by the payments from successful clients it's a viable way to engage and convert new buyers.

An example

The classic example of this would be "no win no fee" solicitors.

Try this:

Depending on your business, if your offering has a definitive result then be bold and charge only once the result is delivered.
If you don't want to offer this to every client, then it can be a great negotiation tool to use strategically in negotiations where it could make the difference between making the sale and not.

See also:

- How to Engage > Loss Aversion
- How to Convert> The Buy Now Pay Later Effect
- How to Convert > Zero Risk Bias
- How to Convert > The No Brainer Effect
- How to Convert > Money Back Guarantee

The Loss Leader Effect

- *Short term loss encourages long term profit.*

What is it?

The Loss Leader Effect is an offering sold below cost to attract buyers.

Why does it work?

It works because buyers can spot a great deal when they see one. Even if a buyer knows you are working at a loss to try and sell them more in the future, it creates an attractive proposition. Having a Loss Leader can be an alternative to a Freemium model where buyers access your offering in a basic form for free. Sometimes being free can damage the perception of value, so having a low-priced offering- even one at a loss - can highlight clients who have a greater lifetime value and the likelihood of buying.

How can you use it?

Create an offering that is as low in price as possible, but that will establish a longer-term relationship with your brand and lead to future, higher value sales.

An example

Amazon have pioneered loss leaders by selling books at a loss via Amazon.com. Attracting buyers with the cheapest books possible- even those which are sold at a loss - creates a relationship and encourages you to buy other things in the store which more than make up for the loss.
It's a bold strategy but for Amazon it has helped to establish their dominance.

Try this:

Identify an entry-level offering that will demonstrate the value you can deliver and encourage a buyer to buy more in the long term. Discount that as low as possible, even below cost, to attract buyers into your product/service ecosystem.

Because the Loss Leader Effect involves trading at a loss it must be used with **EXTREME CAUTION** and sparingly to prevent long term costly issues.

See also:

- How to Get Attention > Freemium
- How to Convert > The Bare Minimum Effect
- How to Convert > The First Purchase Effect

Money Back Guarantee

- *100% results or your money back.*

What is it?

A Money Back Guarantee is one of the most classic and easily implemented ways to encourage client conversion by covering the downside.

Why does it work?

It works because it eliminates risk and demonstrates the confidence the seller has in their offering. A Money Back Guarantee is a strong indicator of a proven offering and a results-driven seller.

How can you use it?

Depending on your offering, identify the result or deliverable your clients are seeking and then provide the assurance that should that result not be achieved, the client can have a refund. This doesn't work for all offerings and can leave you open to some abuse so needs to be used with caution and diligence.

An example

There are countless money back guarantees in the marketplace at any one time, but

Try this:

Be bold. Your offering should deliver what it says it will deliver, so why not make the bold move of offering guarantees to your buyers? The likelihood of refunds is often quite low, but the improvement in conversion is tangible.
Stand by your offering, define the deliverables and guarantee them.

See also:

- How to Convert > Zero Risk Bias
- How to Convert > The No Brainer Effect
- How to Convert > The Promise Effect
- How to Convert > The Pay on Results Effect

The Ready to Use Effect

- ***Give your clients EVERYTHING they need.***

What is it?

The Ready to Use Effect is about ensuring you give your client everything to meet their needs within your offering. It's "washed and ready to eat" salad or premixed screen wash for your car.

Why does it work?

It works because as humans we gravitate towards the path of least resistance. By providing everything a client would need in your offering, you can not only stand out against the competition but can also make bolder claims as to the results and deliverables.

Your clients aren't necessarily looking for the *cheapest* option- they are looking for the easiest and most comprehensive. By offering everything your client needs and focussing on the convenience and directness of results you can sell a "more expensive" option to a client.

How can you use it?

Depending on your offering, identify everything your client will need to meet their needs and combine it into your offering. This might mean a partnership, a larger or more expensive version of your offering. That's OK.
For this model, we are moving away from price and looking at value. If you can confidently tell a potential client you have everything they need and have done the legwork for them, suddenly the price is less of an issue...

An example

The simplest example would pre-washed or pre-prepared food. We pay more for salads, meals and vegetables that are washed, prepared and "ready to use" even if it's more expensive because we value the convenience.

Try this:

Identify what else clients might need to make your offering "work" and bundle that into your offer. Do they need safety gear? Special equipment? Batteries? Ensuring a client has everything they need to use your offering immediately speaks volumes about your commitment to their result.

See also:

- How people Work > Path of Least Resistance
- How people Work > Sell the Destination
-

- Communication Basics > Confidence. Certainty. Expertise
- How to Convert > The Ready to Use Effect

How to <u>lose</u> the sale

To make the sale, you need to know how to lose the sale.

Whilst there is a world of possibility in terms of positive and constructive communication with your target clients... you will witness and be tempted to indulge in lazy and ineffective tactics because you think perhaps this is what you "should" be doing.

From spamming your offer to being pushy and more there are a few cardinal sins that you will have made and will observe in others.

Everything that follows will damage your relationships, your credibility and the opportunity to sell.

.... It's time to lose the sale(!)

The Spam Effect

- *Promoting your offer when it's not relevant or welcome.*

Promoting your offer at every turn- when it's not relevant or called for - is both annoying and disrespectful. Spamming clients puts your needs as the seller ahead of the buyer and is thus poorly received by potential buyers.

Spamming occurs online and offline as well as in conversation. If you find yourself wittering on about your offering despite not being asked any questions, then you are in danger of spamming. Wait for questions or some indication of interest to be sure.

The Pushy Effect

- ***Don't push your clients, you might push them away...***

If you've ever been followed around a shop and continuously asked "if you need any help" then this one is for you.

Being pushy is about putting yourself as the seller first which is suicide in terms of selling. Buyers care about themselves and their needs first, so it makes sense for you to lead

If you feel the urge to "push" for the sale or "touch base" then you need to lead with value and seek to give to the client, not take. Or better yet, find more potential clients. When you have more options, there's less pressure.

The Critical Effect

- ***No-one likes to be criticised. Even if they know they're wrong.***

Although you aren't expected to agree with everything your clients say and do, actively criticizing them can damage your relationship and the sale.

Selling relies on basic trust and respect to work, whilst it's OK to oppose an opinion, you need to be tactful in your communication rather than accusatory.

Some useful phrases:

- Have you thought about...
- I actually thought this was the case...
- I respect your opinion on that...
- I think we both have different viewpoints...

The Dishonesty Effect

- ***If you lie. You lose.***

Telling lies has no place in the selling environment.

Psychology of price

Three isn't always the magic number…

As logical as we might like to think we are, using different numbers in pricing can evoke different things.

Pricing can be used to achieve three distinct objectives:

Make your offering appear "better value"
Notice that's "better value" and not "cheap". You're offering might be "cheap"

Make the buying process simpler.
Following the principle of The Path of Least Resistance, anything that can be done to make the price seem less scary or big can only be a positive thing.

Here we explore simple ways to influence how buyers perceive your pricing.

99.99 and 100.00

So called "charm pricing" makes us think things are cheaper. £2.99 is deemed much cheaper than £3.00 because it starts with a "2" and not a "3" thus we anchor the "2".

How to use it

Remove pennies for emotionally driven purchases (£100)
Add pennies for rational purchases (£99.99)

2 for 1
3 for 2
Buy one get one free

These tactics are used to encourage a sale by not altering the price itself, but altering the *perception* of price as you are receiving more goods for the same price.

Comparative Pricing

By placing expensive things next to cheaper things, you encourage buyers to compare and make their decision

How to use it

Place expensive offerings next to cheaper offerings to make them seem even more reasonable.

Less syllables = easier to process

Pricing with fewer syllables is easier to process. Even if a price is the same length and just one number different, it can affect how buyers process the price and form an unnecessary barrier.
Try this - £22.10 vs £22.17. Twenty-Two Ten (Four syllables) vs. Twenty-Two Seventeen (Six syllables)

How to use it

Use numbers with less syllables where possible to make pricing seem simpler.

Smaller font = smaller price

It's been found that clients perceive your pricing to be smaller if you display it in a smaller font.

£10 vs £10

No comma = smaller price

It's also been found that clients perceive your pricing to be smaller if you remove the commas: £1999 vs £1,999

Partitioned pricing

Separating postage costs or other elements allows you to display a lower price (like the Price Per Use Effect) and thus anchor the buyer to a lower number.

£54.99 Inc. shipping vs. £47.00 + shipping

Instalments

By offering finance in the first place you can engage buyers (The Finance Effect) but it also allows you to anchor to a lower number and make the purchase seem better value.

£9,999 vs £99 per month

How to use it
Promote the smaller monthly figure to make your offering feel more affordable.

Product then price = Luxury items
Price then product = Budget items

When you actually display the price itself plays a role in how it's perceived. It's recommended to display price first for lower value more rational purchases and to display it last for more luxury items.

How to use it
For luxury items, promote the product then the price.
For budget items, promote the price, then the product.

Show the saving contrast

For discounted offerings and sales, you can display the saving as a percentage or a £
It's best to use the largest number possible to make the saving seem larger – save 35% is better than save £1. For higher priced items the actual amount will exceed the % as % is limited to 100.

How to use it

Under £100 use a percentage
Over £100 use the actual amount

Remove currency symbol

Simplifying the price by removing the currency symbol has been proven to make the buying decision easier. A currency symbol reminds the buyer of the "pain" of spending money.

£200 vs 200

Easy to understand discounts.

For discounts, it's best to use the simplest numbers possible – a buyer can understand a 25% discount far quicker than a 23.4% discount

---

Delay payment

If a client has ZERO to pay right now it can soften the blow of the purchase and make it easier for them to convert.

See Also:
How to Convert > The Buy Now Pay Later Effect.

Psychology of colour

Different colours evoke different emotions.

It's difficult to talk about colour and its impact in a black and white or digital copy of this book, but as well as the psychological factors that influence your buyer such as WYSIWYG and The Path of Least Resistance.

There are entire books dedicated to this topic so we can't wish to cover every nuance but it makes sense to be aware of the very basic implications of colour in your sales messaging.

1. Red
Red is the colour of power. It's used to seize and hold attention.
- **Strength, Power, Anxiety, Excitement**

2. Blue
Blue is the colour of trust. It's used to convey stability and security.
- **Calm, Comfort, Logic, Trust**

3. Pink
Pink is the colour of femininity. It's used to appeal to a feminine audience.
- **Gentle, Nurturing, Soft, Tranquil**

4. Yellow

Yellow is the colour of confidence. It's used to portray boldness and confidence.

- **Confidence, Creativity, Happiness, Optimism**

5. Green

Green is the colour of nature. It's used to reference natural offerings and focus on health and wellbeing.

Green is also the colour of acceptance and safety. It's used to highlight the safe choice.

- **Nature, Harmony, Health, Hope**

6. Purple

Purple is the colour of royalty. It's used to portray sophistication, quality and dignity.

- **Luxury, Exclusivity, Quality, Sophistication**

7. Orange

Orange is the colour of energy. It's used to portray youth and dynamism.

- **Fun, Happiness, Liveliness, Happiness**

8. Brown

Brown is the colour of the earth. It's used to portray stability and ruggedness.

- **Nature, Ruggedness, Dependable, Discreet**

9. Black

Black is the colour of elegance. It's used to portray sophistication and quality.

- **Safety, Security, Dignity, Elegance**

10. White

White is the colour of purity. It's used to portray calmness and simplicity.

- **Peace, Purity, Serenity, Honesty**

You're wise to understand the implications of the colours you use in your branding and messaging.

It's possible to say the right things but for your clients to not "feel" right about buying- for example they don't associate Pink with an investment bank.

How to apply this stuff in real life

This is just information...

...what are you going to do with it?

As you've purchased a book about understanding buyer behaviour, it's fair to say you have a definitive objective in mind, so before we get to the myriad of different things you need to know, I have collated shortcuts to help you achieve your goals.

Firstly, you will notice the book is split into three distinctive sections;

- How to Get Attention
- How to Engage
- How to Convert

Whatever you are trying to accomplish in business, it should fall into these broad categories, but to make this book as useful a tool as possible, there are a number of other potential circumstances you may be facing which are listed below and categorised as:

- Communicating your offering
- Selling your offering.

Each section is designed to be actionable and links to the relevant parts of the book to help you achieve your objective.

Communicating your offering

Communicating your offering is where every part of the sales process begins.

Everything at Clear Sales Message is built on the notion that:

"If they don't understand it. They can't buy it."

There are seven core questions we need to consider and to answer in our messaging to maximise our chances of engagement and understanding:

Question 1: What do you do?
Question 2: How can you help me? (why should I care?)
Question 3: Why should I choose you?
Question 4: How much does it cost?
Question 5: How will I know I need you?
Question 6: How will I remember you?
Question 7: How will I describe you to others?

In this section, we look at 8 distinct milestones that you will face when communicating your offering and link those to the approaches you need to get the result you want:

1. Launching a new product or service
2. How to reach more new potential clients
3. How to differentiate from the competition
4. How to increase website/advert conversions
5. How to be more memorable
6. How to explain your offering more clearly
7. How to increase visibility on social media
8. How to gain client trust

Launching a new product or service

From being seen, to being sold.

Launching a new product or service demands that you have both the attention and understanding of your audience.
From offering free gifts to incentivising a first purchase and offering free samples; there are seven ways you can maximise your chances of being noticed and understood.

How People Work	> The Abundance Effect
Communications Basics	> The Timely Effect
How to Get Attention	> Freemium
How to Convert	> The Prize Draw Effect
How to Convert	> Zero Risk Bias
How to Convert	> The Free Gift Effect
How to Convert	> The First Purchase Effect
How to Convert	> The Mini Pack Effect
How to Convert	> The Bare Minimum Effect
How to Convert	> The Loss Leader Effect
How to Convert	> Money Back Guarantee
How to Convert	> The Pay on Results Effect

How to reach more new potential clients

Keeping the funnel topped up.

Reaching new clients with an existing offering is the mainstay of "sales" departments in every company.
But how do you physically make contact or encourage contact with new potential clients?

How to Get Attention	> Freemium
How to Get Attention	> Propinquity
How to Engage	> Lead Magnet
How to Engage Content Effect	> The User Generated
How to Engage	> Trigger Point
How to Convert	> The Prize Draw Effect
How to Convert	> The Free Gift Effect
How to Convert	> Refer a friend Effect
How to Convert Effect	> The Buy Now Pay Later

How to differentiate from the competition

If they can't see you, they can't buy it.

Being forgettable is expensive, but being indistinguishable from the competition is potentially worse.

Here we look at this is how you can stand out and be noticed.

How People Work	> The Established Effect.
Communications Basics Effect	> The Facts and Figures
How to Get Attention	> The Named Process Effect
How to Get Attention	> The Controversy Effect
How to Get Attention	> The Signature Effect
How to Get Attention	> The Tagline Effect
How to Get Attention	> The Award-Winning Effect
How to Engage	> The Exclusive Effect
How to Engage	> The Good Cause Effect
How to Engage	> The "I have a Dream" Effect
How to Engage	> The Speed Effect
How to Engage	> The Personification Effect
How to Convert	> Social Proof
How to Convert	> The Pay on Results Effect
How to Convert	> Money Back Guarantee
How to Convert	> The Ready to Use Effect

How to Increase website / advert conversions

Converting attention is the name of the game...

Converting attention once you have it has a lot do with simplicity of communication as well as demonstrating confidence, certainty and expertise.

Here we look at how we provide buyers with the information they need to make their decision.

How People Work	> Overchoice
How People Work	> Path of Least Resistance
Communication Basics	> Inverted Pyramid
Communication Basics	> Facts and figures
How to Get Attention	> The Show and Tell Effect
How to Engage	> Destination/journey
How to Engage	> First Person Questions
How to Engage	> The Story Effect
How to Engage	> The Empathy Effect

How to be more memorable

Being forgettable is expensive...

Here we look at some simple ways to communicate and interact with your potential clients in a more memorable way,

How to Get Attention	> The Bizarreness Effect
How to Get Attention	> The Named Process Effect
How to Get Attention	> The Controversy Effect
How to Get Attention	> The Sex Effect
How to Get Attention	> The Signature Effect
How to Get Attention	> The Humour Effect
How to Get Attention	> The Tagline Effect
How to Engage	> The "I have a Dream" Effect
How to Engage	> The Personification Effect
How to Engage	> The Education Effect
How to Engage	> Lagniappe

In addition to this, creating a memorable and engaging tagline can help to be remembered: www.howtowriteatagline.com

How to explain your offering more clearly

If they don't understand it. They can't buy it.

Being able to clearly explain your offering is a vital and often overlooked element of sales. Whether you have a simple or complicated offering, here we look at some simple ways to be clear and understood.

How People Work	> WYSIWYG
How People Work	> Sell the destination.
Communication Basics	> The Burden of Proof
Communication Basics	> Inverted Pyramid
Communication Basics	> The Framing Effect
How to Get Attention	> The Repetition Effect
How to Get Attention	> The Before /After Effect
How to Get Attention	> The Named Process Effect
How to Engage	> Equivalence
How to Engage	> The Story Effect
How to Convert	> The Ready to Use Effect

In addition to this, you may wish to consider addressing your overall sales messaging which can be found here – www.clearsalesmessage.com/book

How to increase visibility on social media

Turning fans and followers into sales and conversions.

Seizing attention is tricky. With so many social media posts, accounts, real world advertising and television vying for attention it can be hard to stand out.
Here we look at some simple ways to be noticed and/or to encourage others to share your content and spark conversation.

Communication Basics   > The Timely Effect
How to Get Attention   > The Sex Effect
How to Get Attention   > The Controversy Effect
How to Get Attention   > The Hashtag Effect
How to Get Attention   > The Like & Share Effect
How to Get Attention   > The Bizarreness Effect
How to Get Attention   > Propinquity
How to Get Attention   > The Humour Effect
How to Engage   > Lead Magnet
How to Engage   > The User Generated
Content Effect

How to gain client trust

Before anyone buys from you, they must first trust you.

Trust is a combination of credibility and reliability. You start building trust (or not) with clients from the very first interaction.
These methods specifically address credibility and reliability in your messaging.

How people work	> The Authority Effect
Communication Basics	> Facts and figures
Communication Basics	> The Honesty Effect
How to Get Attention	> The Named Process Effect
How to Get Attention	> The Award-Winning Effect
How to Engage	> First Person Questions
How to Engage	> The Scoring Effect
How to Convert	> Social Proof
How to Convert	> The Qualify Effect
How to Convert	> Zero Risk Bias
How to Convert	> The Pay on Results Effect
How to Convert	> Money Back Guarantee
How to Convert	> The Ready to Use Effect

Selling your offering

When it comes to actually "selling" your offering, how do you move someone from browsing to buying?

In this section, we look at 7 distinct milestones that you will face when selling your offering and link those to the approaches you need to get the result you want:

1. How to sell more to new clients
2. How to sell more to existing clients
3. How to encourage repeat business
4. How to encourage referrals
5. How to re-engage prospects who didn't buy
6. How to sell more of an underperforming offering
7. How to sell higher priced items.

How to sell more to new clients

If they're going to be buying anyway, they might as well buy BIG.

If you want to maximise the volume / price point at which you sell to new clients, there are some simple methods to deploy. You will be familiar with a number of them and will have purchased more yourself as a result.

How people work	> The "In for a Penny" Effect
How people work	> The Treat Effect
How to Get Attention	> The Price Per Use Effect
How to Engage	> Anchoring
How to Engage	> The Premium Effect
How to Engage	> The Repurposing Effect
How to Engage	> The Exclusive Effect
How to Convert	> The Points Effect
How to Convert	> The Loyalty Effect
How to Convert	> The Buy More Effect
How to Convert	> The Deal Effect
How to Convert	> The Finance Effect How to
How to Convert	> The Pay on Results Effect
How to Convert	> The Mega Pack Effect
How to Convert	> The With-Purchase Effect
How to Convert	> Money Back Guarantee

How to sell more to existing clients

It's easier to sell more to people who have already bought.

Selling to existing clients is "easier" as you already have trust and have proven what your offering delivers. These simple methods make it as easy as possible for clients to buy again.

How People Work	> The "In for a Penny" Effect
How to Engage	> The Repurposing Effect
How to Engage	> The Exclusive Effect
How to Convert	> The Buy More Effect
How to Convert	> The Finance Effect
How to Convert	> The Mega Pack Effect
How to Convert	> The With-Purchase Effect

How to encourage repeat business

You don't want to be in the selling business, you want to be in the _re-ordering_ business...

As it's "easier" to sell to existing clients, it makes sense to create a situation or system that allows them to order repeatedly from you and in volume. Making it easier to buy more and buy again means they are more likely to buy more and buy again.

How to Get Attention	> New Version Effect
How to Engage	> The Repurposing Effect
How to Engage	> Lagniappe
How to Convert	> The Points Effect
How to Convert	> The Loyalty Effect
How to Convert	> The Subscription Effect
How to Convert	> The With-Purchase Effect
How to Convert	> The Ready to Use Effect

How to encourage referrals

Referred prospects are the highest converting type of prospect.

Referrals are based on trust (credibility + reliability). Focussing on the personal recommendation and incentivising sharing drives referred business.

How to Get Attention	> The Like & Share Effect
How to Engage	> The identity effect
How to Engage	> Law of Reciprocity
How to Convert	> The Free Gift Effect
How to Convert	> The refer a friend effect
How to Convert	> The Pay on Results Effect
How to Convert	> Money Back Guarantee

How to re-engage prospects who didn't buy

The fortune's in the follow up.

It's often reported that sales can take as many as 8 or more follow ups to be made. Whilst there are no hard facts about how many times to follow up and re-engage, here we explore some methods to re-ignite sales conversations.

How to Get Attention	> Freemium
How to Get Attention	> The New Version Effect
How to Get Attention	> The Events effect
How to Get Attention	> The Price Per Use Effect
How to Engage	> The Education Effect
How to Engage	> Trigger Point
How to Convert	> The Prize Draw Effect
How to Convert	> The Free Gift Effect
How to Convert	> The First Purchase Effect
How to Convert	> The Mega Pack Effect
How to Convert	> The Mini Pack Effect
How to Convert	> The Pay on Results Effect
How to Convert	> Money Back Guarantee

How to sell more of an underperforming offering

If you promote it. They will come...

When an offering underperforms, it might be that you need to not only draw additional attention to it, but also to be much clearer on the benefits as your potential buyers may not understand or engage with just how good it is.

How to Get Attention	> The New Version Effect
How to Get Attention	> The Events Effect
How to Engage	>The Eco Effect
How to Convert	> The Checklist Effect
How to Convert	> The Price Match Effect
How to Convert	> The Comparison Effect
How to Convert	> The Also Bought Effect
How to Convert	> The Mega Pack Effect
How to Convert	> The Points effect
How to Convert	> The Prize Draw Effect
How to Convert	> The Loss Leader Effect
How to Convert	> The Pay on Results Effect
How to Convert	> Money Back Guarantee

How to sell higher priced items

Expensive is relative...

Selling "higher priced" items can often come down to the confidence of the sales person themselves and whether or not they can afford what they are selling.

How People Work	> Sell the destination
Communication Basics	> The Framing Effect
How to Get Attention	> The Price per use effect
How to Engage	> Equivalence
How to Engage	> The Repurposing Effect
How to Engage	> The Premium effect
How to Convert	> The Qualify Effect
How to Convert	> The Finance Effect
How to Convert Effect	> The Buy Now Pay Later
How to Convert	> The Pay on Results Effect
How to Convert	> Money Back Guarantee
How to Convert	> The Ready to Use Effect

See also: Psychology of Price

The numbers you use in your pricing can have an impact on your buyer and drive their engagement and decision making - especially if the offering is "expensive".

What now?

Good question.

There is a LOT to take on board in this book, all of it has a place in the selling environment but not all of it will be relevant to you in the here and now.

This book is both a resource and a source of learning. Whilst there are parts of the book you can action immediately - whether you are looking to capture your client's attention, engage them or convert them to a sale- there is a larger part of the book that forms the basis of your selling "general knowledge".

Keep this book to hand when you are selling, advertising and creating or launching new offerings; it will provide you with the ideas, inspiration and insight you need to maximise every opportunity.

When you see advertising, messaging or any form of selling, you should be able to breakdown into components precisely what is happening and why. This understanding allows you to not only make better decisions as a buyer, but to also incorporate these new findings when you are selling.

This book was written with those people in mind who claim they "hate selling" or that they "don't know how to sell."

It's hoped that armed with this vital information and understanding about the basics of communication that many of the unknowns and sources of anxiety will be eradicated.

Did you enjoy this book?

Thank you for buying this book.

If you'd like to leave a review (positive or negative) on Amazon, please do so as we value your opinion.

Thank you.

Success Stories

We love to hear about the successes our clients and readers enjoy; if you use this book and subsequently experience success in your business we would love to hear from you.

Please email success@clearsalesmessage.com

Also from James Newell:

- **What are you selling?**
- **Who are you selling it to?**
- **...and why should they care?**

If you aren't clear on this, your sales efforts will be severely limited.

The Clear Sales Message book focusses on the **7 core questions** your clients will be thinking or asking prior to making any purchase from you.

Remember: if they don't understand it. They can't buy it.

www.clearsalesmessage.com/book

Also from
James Newell:

8 seconds.

That's all the time you have.

When communicating with new potential clients, you have 8 seconds of their attention.

In 8 seconds, you need to **grab attention**, **explain what you do** and **generate enough interest** that the potential client may wish to know more.

Oh, and you need to **be memorable** too. In 8 seconds.

To achieve this- you need a tagline.

www.howtowriteatagline.com

Also from James Newell:

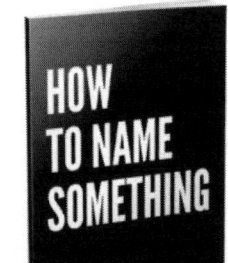

Don't give yourself a bad name.

The name of your business, product or service is one of the **most crucial** and yet **most overlooked** elements.

So many businesses, products and services have **forgettable** or **difficult to read and remember** names.

Your name is your **first impression**. It's crucial.

www.howtonamesomething.com

Also from James Newell:

What makes your buyers buy?

"80+ ways to reach, engage and convert people to buy using psychology, science and common sense."

In the book, we cover:

How people work – 18+ factors that affect client behaviour.
Communication Basics – 12+ ways to communicate more clearly.
How to Get Attention – 18+ ways to stand out and be noticed.
How to engage – 27+ ways to engage potential buyers.
How to convert – 10 ways to convert prospects to buyers.
Everything in the book works and is **backed by psychology, science, common sense and our own testing.**

www.understandyourbuyer.com

Start using Email as a <u>SELLING TOOL</u>

- How to get your emails **noticed.**
- How to get your emails **opened**.
- How to get your emails **acted upon.**

When you realise that **every Email you send is an advert** for your business and that every Email you send is **an opportunity to sell**, you start to see email for what it is. A SELLING TOOL.

EMAIL KIT is **a self-paced online course** that gives you everything you need to ensure **every email you send is optimised to sell** using the CLEAR SALES MESSAGE principles.

<u>www.emailkit.co.uk</u>

Maximise <u>EVERY</u> networking opportunity

- How to **introduce yourself** effectively.
- What to say in your "**pitch**".
- How to be more **memorable & engaging.**

Networking is one of the most cost-effective ways to find new business, but there's a problem: **Just what do you say when you network?** From introducing yourself to the dreaded "pitch" section, knowing what to say can make the difference between networking and "not working".

NETWORKING PITCH KIT is **a self-paced online course** that gives you everything you need to ensure **every interaction you have at a networking event is optimised to sell** using the CLEAR SALES MESSAGE principles.

www.networkingpitchkit.com

Printed in Great Britain
by Amazon